Hans Dieter Schaal

Scenic Architecture
Szenische Architektur

Hans Dieter Schaal
Scenic Architecture
Szenische Architektur

with a preface by
mit einem Vorwort von
Frank R. Werner

Edition Axel Menges

ISBN 978-3-936681-97-0

Printing and binding / Druck und Bindearbeiten: Graspo CZ, a.s., Zlín, Czech Republic / Tschechische Republik

Translation into English / Übersetzung ins Englische: Alison Kirkland
Book design / Buchgestaltung: Axel Menges

Picture on the backside of the jacket / Bild auf der Rückseite des Umschlags: Hans Dieter Schaal, 1989. (Photo: Blum.)

Contents

Inhalt

Frank Rolf Werner

From mental mapping to the cartography of »other« spatial landscapes. Some remarks on the scenographic work of Hans Dieter Schaal

The scenically staged presentation of objects or proceedings in private and public spaces is probably as old as humankind itself. Whether created for cultic, political, or prestige-related reasons, the scenes in question would always possess a special aura; an aura that clearly distinguished them from other art forms. For there can be no question that these ambitious presentations of significant objects or theatrical proceedings amounted to art, and even to a high art. Notwithstanding this, the spectacular scenic presentations that took place over the millennia are known to us only from historical descriptions. It was not until the Italian Renaissance that the creators of these object and space configurations emerged from the anonymity of historical reports. In the »Liber Secundus« of his treatise *De Architectura Libri Quinque* (1569), Sebastiano Serlio discusses the subject of perspective, and gives a detailed description of the effect produced by three exemplary city and landscape spaces, scenically composed and represented in woodcuts. He describes these as representing the »scena comica«, the »scena tragica«, and the »scena satyrica«. In her 2005 study *Das Drama des Sehens: Auge, Blick und Bühnenform*, Ulrike Haas spoke of the epoch-making significance of the three staging types: »Serlio brings the social differentiation of the genres into the foreground. The *scena comica* is actually exclusively determined by its social aspect, thereby placing it at the centre of the genres. In the guise of the tripartite division (as adopted by Vitruvius) this affects a shifting and reversal of the genre hierarchy: the most elevated form, the *scena tragica,* continues to be described as such, but no longer plays the role of the first and foremost genre. ... Serlio's *scena comica* is not characterised by a low style of architecture and a lack of symmetrical beauty. Instead, these everyday buildings are inhabited by a spirit that ›never wishes to place the considerations of usefulness after the considerations of pleasure‹, as Alberti writes. For this reason, the comic stage is shown as a complete, self-contained world. It is no longer simply a district, but a whole world on a small scale – and it is inhabited by living bodies.«

A *scena comica* of this kind was built at Vicenza, in Italy. In the year 1580, Andrea Palladio drew the plans for the first permanent theatre building of the modern age: the Teatro Olimpico. Although it was not completed until after his death, the permanently installed stage set – an ideal city – continues to this day to dominate the theatre's interior, which is scenically composed as a unified artwork in its own right, regardless of time and space. During the Italian and European baroque period, staged scenes of all kinds experienced a positive boom. An abundance of accounts of spectacular temporary displays and decorative compositions survive from this era. They were conceived and implemented for coronations, marriages, funerals, peace accords or other political events, and took place in public plazas and streets, and in private spaces. In the realm of theatres and opera houses, artists and stage architects like Giuseppe Galli da Bibiena and others succeeded in applying the refinements of their scene-creating arts, which burst the bounds of space by setting their sights on infinity, to the architecture of their age. And Giovanni Battista Piranesi's *Carceri,* obsessively fascinating as they lose themselves in abysses, were even included in imposing *veduta* compilations such as the collection of stage sets entitled *Raccolta di prospettive serie, rustiche, e di paesaggio*, offered to the public by Antonio Basoli in 1810 in Bologna.

However, it was the multitalented Karl Friedrich Schinkel who was to prove to be the most effective 19th-century impresario of staged-scene objects and found pieces, spaces and architectural features. Works created by him, such as the Pfaueninsel, the Schlosspark in Glienicke and the Charlottenhof in Potsdam prove that almost all of his works feature a seemingly effortless combining of heterogeneous fields, such as consumer goods design, furniture construction, interior architecture, architecture, painting, stage set design, garden design, urban construction, and preservation of historic structures. The mentality of the unified, composed scene that is the thread running through Schinkel's work anticipates, as it were, the verdict of Hans Hollein who, in 1967, coined the slogan: »everything is architecture«.

Among the early 20th-century avant-gardes, the idea of all-embracing staged scenes fell on particularly fertile ground in the context of Russian revolutionary architecture and Italian Futurism. After all, both movements were inherently concerned with the toppling of old political systems and the establishing of a more revolutionary concept of culture that would be closer to the people. This led to the Russian »Proletkult« initiative headed by Anatoly Vasilyevich Lunacharsky, which, in terms of quality and quantity, represented the most impressive and extensive exercise in agitprop scene-creation of the whole 20th century. Every form of media and materials the epoch had to offer were used to transform whole plaza ensembles, streetscapes, and public buildings into visualisations of new social provenances – sometimes even set into dramatic motion. Kinetic constructivist stage sets such as the work of Alexandra Exter and other Soviet Russian artists, viewed today, have lost nothing of their experimental impetus. Even Mussolini's Fascists, in staging their exhibitions such as *Mostra della Rivoluzione fascista,* made use of the scene-creation arts offered by Futurism – with the associated furore.

Even the German avant-garde, despite their reputation of being purist, produced Kurt Schwitters' *Merzbau*, a space-encompassing and space-transcending scenically-composed assemblage that was the only one of its kind in Europe. Herbert Bayer attracted much attention with his »Section allemande« scenic creation for the *Expositon de la société des artistes décorateurs* at the Paris Grand Palais in 1930. Later, Bayer wrote that: »Traditionally, the only direction of gaze that existed in an exhibition was the horizontal direction. Here (in Paris), new possibilities for expanding the field of vision were being experimented with, so that the non-horizontal surfaces could also be exploited; this revealed whole new aspects ... such as an enlarging of the field of vision, with an associated enlarging of creative possibilities.« Panoptical rooms with their dynamic polarity reversed, with »displays« hung at an angle within the space, and elevated standpoints, surrounded by seemingly flying or floating exhibits, were a source of lasting astonishment among art expert circles.

After the end of the Second World War – following the theatrically ostentatious but also outspokenly suggestive mass spectacles staged by the National Social-

Frank Rolf Werner

Vom Mental Mapping zur Kartographie »anderer« Raumlandschaften. Anmerkungen zu den szenographischen Arbeiten von Hans Dieter Schaal

Das inszenierte Präsentieren von Objekten oder Handlungen in privaten und öffentlichen Räumen dürfte so alt sein wie die Menschheit. Ob aus kultischen, politischen oder repräsentativen Beweggründen heraus entstanden, stets kam den jeweiligen Inszenierungen eine besondere Aura zu; eine Aura, die sie deutlich von anderen Kunstformen abhob. Denn daß es sich bei ambitionierten Präsentationen bedeutender Objekte oder theatralischer Vorgänge um eine Kunst, ja sogar eine hohe Kunst handelte, stand außer Frage. Gleichwohl waren uns spektakuläre Inszenierungen über Jahrtausende hinweg nur aus historischen Beschreibungen bekannt. Erst mit der italienischen Renaissance traten die Schöpfer derartiger Objekt- oder Raumkonfigurationen aus der Anonymität historischer Rapporte hervor. So geht Sebastiano Serlio im »Liber Secundus« seiner Abhandlung *De Architectura Libri Quinque* (1569) beim Thema Perspektive ausführlich auf die Wirkung von drei exemplarisch inszenierten und in Holzschnitten dargestellten Stadt- und Landschaftsräumen ein. Er bezeichnet diese als »Scena comica«, »*Scena tragica*« und »Scena satyrica«. Ulrike Haas hat 2005 in ihrer Studie *Das Drama des Sehens: Auge, Blick und Bühnenform* auf die epochale Bedeutung der drei typisierten Inszenierungen hingewiesen: »Serlio rückt die soziale Differenzierung der Gattungen in den Vordergrund. Der soziale Aspekt bestimmt die *Scena comica* sogar ausschließlich und setzt sie dadurch ins Zentrum der Gattungen. Dies bewirkt im Gewand der von Vitruv übernommenen Dreiteilung eine Umschichtung der Hierarchien der Gattungen, deren erhabenste, die *Scena tragica*, zwar weiterhin als solche behauptet wird, jedoch nicht mehr die erste Rolle unter den Gattungen spielt. ... Nicht der niedere Stil der Architektur und der Mangel an schöner Symmetrie zeichnet Serlios *Scena comica* aus, sondern daß in ihren alltäglichen Bauten ein Geist wohnt, der ›nie die Erwägungen der Nützlichkeit dem Vergnügen hintangesetzt wissen will‹, wie Alberti schreibt. Die komische Bühne wird aus diesem Grund als eine vollständige und in sich abschließbare Welt gezeigt. Sie ist nicht mehr nur ein Bezirk, sondern eine ganze Welt im Kleinen – und sie wird von lebendigen Leibern bewohnt.«

Gebaut wurde eine solche *Scena comica* im italienischen Vicenza. Im Jahr 1580 zeichnete Andrea Palladio die Pläne für den ersten festen Theaterbau der Neuzeit, das Teatro Olimpico. Obgleich erst nach seinem Tode ausgeführt, beherrscht sein dauerhaft installiertes Bühnenbild in Gestalt einer idealen Stadt bis heute den Innenraum des auch in seiner Gänze als Gesamtkunstwerk inszenierten Interieurs jenseits von Zeit und Raum. Im italienischen und europäischen Barock erlebten Inszenierungen jedweder Art schließlich eine regelrechte Hochblüte. In Bild und Wort sind uns aus dieser Zeit prachtvolle temporäre Zurschaustellungen und Dekorationen in Fülle überliefert, welche aufgrund von Krönungen, Hochzeiten, Begräbnissen, Friedensschlüssen oder anderen politischen Ereignissen für öffentliche Plätze, Straßen oder private Räume konzipiert und ausgeführt wurden. Auf dem Terrain der Theater und Opernhäuser waren es Künstler und Bühnenarchitekten wie Giuseppe Galli da Bibiena und andere, die das Raffinement ihrer raumsprengenden, weil ins Unendliche zielenden Inszenierungskünste sogar auf die Architektur ihrer Zeit zu übertragen wußten. Und Giovanni Battista Piranesis obsessiv faszinierende, sich in Abgründe verlierende *Carceri* fanden selbst noch Eingang in so prachtvolle Vedutenwerke wie etwa die Bühnenbildsammlung *Raccolta di prospettive serie, rustiche, e di paesaggio*, welche Antonio Basoli 1810 der Öffentlichkeit in Bologna vorstellte.

Als wirkungsmächtigster Impressario inszenierter Objekte und Fundstücke, Räume und Architekturen sollte sich im 19. Jahrhundert jedoch das Multitalent Karl Friedrich Schinkel erweisen. Werke von seiner Hand, wie etwa die Pfaueninsel, der Schloßpark in Glienicke oder der Charlottenhof in Potsdam belegen, daß er in nahezu allen seiner Arbeiten heterogene Sparten wie Gebrauchsgüterdesign, Möbelbau, Innenarchitektur, Architektur, Malerei, Bühnenbildnerei, Gartengestaltung, Städtebau und Denkmalpflege scheinbar mühelos zur Deckung bringen konnte. Das ganzheitliche inszenatorische Denken, das Schinkels Werk wie ein roter Faden durchzieht, stellt gleichsam eine Vorwegnahme jenes Verdiktes dar, welches Hans Hollein 1967 mit dem Slogan »Alles ist Architektur« auf den Punkt bringen sollte.

Unter den Avantgarden des frühen 20. Jahrhunderts fiel das Thema allumfassender Inszenierungen vor allem in der russischen Revolutionsarchitektur und im italienischen Futurismus auf fruchtbaren Boden. Verfolgten doch beide Strömungen auf programmatische Weise den Sturz alter politischer Systeme und die Etablierung eines volksnäheren, revolutionären Kulturbegriffs. So hat der russische, von Anatoli Wassiljewitsch Lunatscharski gelenkte »Proletkult«, was Qualität und Quantität anbelangt, die wohl eindrucksvollsten und raumgreifendsten Agitprop-Inszenierungen des gesamten 20. Jahrhunderts hervorgebracht. Unter Verwendung aller seinerzeit verfügbaren Medien und Materialien verwandelten sich dabei ganze Platzensembles, Straßenzüge und öffentliche Bauten in mitunter sogar dramaturgisch bewegte Schaubilder neuer gesellschaftlicher Provenienzen. Kinetische konstruktivistische Bühnenbilder, wie die von Alexandra Exter und anderen sowjetrussischen Künstlerinnen, haben denn auch bis heute nichts von ihrem experimentellen Impetus eingebüßt. Und selbst Mussolinis Faschisten bedienten sich bei ihren Ausstellungen, wie etwa der *Mostra della Rivoluzione fascista*, wie selbstverständlich immer noch des Furors futuristischer Inszenierungskünste.

Sogar die als puristisch verrufene deutsche Avantgarde lieferte mit Kurt Schwitters *Merzbau* eine den Raum um- und ihn weit übergreifende, inszenatorische Assemblage, die ihresgleichen in Europa suchte. Und Herbert Bayer sorgte mit seiner Inszenierung der »Section allemande« im Rahmen der *Expositon de la société des artistes décorateurs* im Pariser Grand Palais 1930 für großes Aufsehen. Bayer schrieb dazu später: »Traditionsgemäß kannte man in Ausstellungen nur die horizontale Blickrichtung. Hier (in Paris) wurde nun mit neuen Möglichkeiten zur Ausweitung des Gesichtsfeldes experimentiert, so daß nicht mehr nur die senkrechten Flächen ausgenützt wurden; dadurch ergaben sich ganz neue Aspekte, ... wie eine Vergrößerung des Gesichtsfeldes und die damit verbundenen Gestaltungsmöglichkeiten.« Dynamisch umgepolte, panoptische Räume mit schräg in den Raum eingehängten »Displays« sowie erhöhte Standpunkte, umgeben von scheinbar fliegenden oder schwebenden Exponaten, setzten die Fachwelt seinerzeit nachhaltig in Erstaunen.

Nach den pompös-theatralischen, aber ausgesprochen suggestiven Massenspektakeln der Nationalsozialisten gerieten Inszenierungen jeglicher Art nach dem Ende des Zweiten Weltkriegs zunehmend ins Abseits. In spar-

ists – staged scenes of any kind became increasingly marginalised. In the new age, the only aura was to be that of the exhibit itself, communicating itself within exhibitions of a Spartan simplicity. This not infrequently led to entirely understandable incomprehension in visitors who were perfectly willing to understand. It was the Austrian architect Hans Hollein who was next able to use powerful and visually strong scenic compositions to create almost joyful scenes, even for exhibitions on such banal subjects as »paper«, »wood«, »glass«, and »ceramics«.

Post-1945 Germany boasted a series of highly-regarded stage set designers, such as Winfried Minks, Jürgen Rose, and Karl-Ernst Herrmann. And yet, in the 1970s, Hans Dieter Schaal succeeded, strikingly and consistently, in becoming a pioneer of a very different kind of stage set culture, by creating sometimes breathtaking visualised »mind mapping« panoramas. In the field of German exhibition architecture, it was the same story. Whilst Claus-Peter Gross continued, for many years, to pursue purist exhibition concepts that remained anchored in the Bauhaus tradition, other exhibition designers, such as Klaus-Jürgen Sembach, made an effort to achieve more suitable spatial configurations, tailored to the exhibits in question. Gottfried Korff offered a very precise analysis of the fundamental paradigm shift in the character of exhibitions in his essay »Zielpunkt: Neue Prächtigkeit? Notizen zur Geschichte kulturhistorischer Ausstellungen in der ›alten‹ Bundesrepublik« (1996). Hans Dieter Schaal played, as it were, a leading role in the inception of this paradigm shift – away from simple presentation of the exhibits selected by the curators and toward complex, scenographically enhanced thought spaces.

The pioneering character and continuing success of Schaal's scenic compositions for stage sets and exhibitions is significantly due to this field allowing him to take full advantage of his multiple talents. He succeeds equally in thinking and working practically as an architect, a painter, a sculptor, a landscape designer, an urban visionary, and a man of literature, and this allows him to discover space-embracing scenographic installations that are unique three-dimensional equivalents for his paper-drawn »thought spaces« and »path spaces« and »thought buildings« from the 1970s. His renowned compendium entitled *Architektonische Situationen*, published in 1980 and containing, as it were, the essence of his early spatial studies, in fact contains within it the seeds of all his later stage set and exhibition configurations.

The symbiotic relationship between legendary director Ruth Berghaus and spatial visionary Schaal first began producing history-making stage sets in the early 1980s. Working with Berghaus, Schaal created elementary spatial compositions possessed of great suggestive power for *Les Troyens* (1983), *Wozzeck* (1984), *Orpheus* (1986), *Elektra* (1986), *Moses und Aron* (1987), *Tristan und Isolde* (1988), *Lulu* (1988), *Fierrabras* (1988), *Ariane et Barbe-Bleue* (1991) and *Nachtwache* (1993), later working with other directors to do the same for countless other operas and theatre pieces. Deconstructed spatial constellations, planes wedged into one another at angles, pieces of architecture with skewed perspective, gigantic planetary bodies, and landscapes as if frozen in ice and the endless depths of space are condensed into dreamlike images, never seen before; images that always expose archaic memories or buried yearnings. Schaal sees himself not as an illustrator of some given scenic event, but as an emancipated scenic choreographer of pictorial tableaux which act in relation to the specific events on stage as additional but hidden plot threads: commenting, interpreting, and conceptually extending.

The same is true of his concepts for temporary and permanent exhibitions. Before undertaking any of the individual projects on his long list of exhibition projects, large and small, Schaal has always researched archive material, historic background, and repercussions, but also the emotional and psychoanalytical implications of the exhibition's themes and the associated exhibits, almost with the meticulousness of a scientific specialist. In works such as his installations for *Berlin – Berlin* (1987) or *Prometheus* (1998), for the Filmmuseum Berlin (2000), and for the memorials of the concentration camps Mittelbau-Dora (2006), Bergen-Belsen (2007), and Esterwegen (2011) he always presents his own view of the world, his own view of things.

Schaal's treatment of exhibits is faintly reminiscent of Schinkel's treatment of spolia in the park at Glienicke; he regards them as found objects from a lost time. He endeavours to isolate these found objects, to estimate and weigh up their cultural and historical value and their impact: in order, ultimately, to assign them a fixed place in his 3D cartographies. Framed by impressive architectonic »tableaux vivants«, exhibits are configured into never before seen dream cities and dream landscapes that one can walk through, that, instead of leaving visitors untouched, encourage them to enter the new »terrain vague« that has been prepared for them – an entirely different one each time. In exploring this terrain, empathy and involvement are sometimes of more value than cognitive knowledge. Thus, Schaal makes the visitors to his exhibitions into members in an expedition, who move along tangled paths as they wander through and experience the »tropics« of his exhibition landscapes.

»The outer appearance of the world, as it is given to my senses« in the words of Michael Hauskeller, »is not by itself sufficient to make the atmospheric experience comprehensible. For me, the world as it is is always more than the plain appearance, it is the appearing world, not a dream, but experienced reality. This something more in the experience, that transcends the plain appearance as a collection of sense data, the aspect of this that contains the world, is the indispensible foundation of the sensing of atmosphere, and it is only through this that appearance achieves its general significance.« Here, Hauskeller is referring to an »in-between«, a state between the real and imagined world. For, he says, this »in-between« is »decisive for my-finding-myself-within-a-world.«

This quality of finding-myself – or rediscovering-myself – within the world may be one of the most important motifs in the spatial installations collected in this volume. In these designs, Schaal has accorded »scenography« a very specific new significance. After all, there is no-one else who achieves this so impressively, this temptation to assimilate the atmosphere of »other« places, this positively sensual temptation to a »different« reading of history – a reading that perhaps lies closer to our own reality.

tanisch einfach gehaltenen Ausstellungen sollte nur noch die Aura des Exponats kommunizieren dürfen. Nicht selten herrschte da freilich verständnislose Ratlosigkeit bei verständniswilligen Betrachtern. Erst dem österreichischen Künstlerarchitekten Hans Hollein sollte es wieder vergönnt sein, Ausstellungen selbst für so scheinbar banale Themen wie »Papier«, »Holz«, »Glas« oder »Keramik« mit Hilfe kraftvoller und bildmächtiger Inszenierungen geradezu lustvoll in Szene zu setzen.

In Deutschland gab es nach 1945 zwar eine Reihe angesehener Bühnenbildner, wie Winfried Minks, Jürgen Rose oder Karl-Ernst Herrmann. Aber dennoch gelang es Hans Dieter Schaal, seit den 1970er Jahren zum ebenso prägenden wie programmatischen Vorreiter einer ganz andersartigen Bühnenbildkultur zu werden, nämlich zu mitunter atemberaubenden Panoramen eines visualisierten »Mind Mapping«. Ähnlich sah es auf dem Terrain der Ausstellungsarchitektur in Deutschland aus. Während Claus-Peter Gross über viele Jahre hinweg puristische, noch ganz in der Tradition des Bauhauses verankerte Ausstellungskonzepte verfolgte, bemühten sich andere Ausstellungsgestalter, wie etwa Klaus-Jürgen Sembach, bereits um adäquatere, den jeweiligen Exponaten angepaßte Raumkonfigurationen. Gottfried Korff hat den grundlegenden Paradigmenwechsel im Ausstellungswesen in seinem Aufsatz »Zielpunkt: Neue Prächtigkeit? Notizen zur Geschichte kulturhistorischer Ausstellungen in der ›alten‹ Bundesrepublik« (1996) sehr präzise analysiert. Diesen Paradigmenwechsel, weg von der einfachen Präsentation der von den jeweiligen Kuratoren ausgewählten Exponate hin zu komplexen, szenographisch überhöhten Denkräumen, hat Hans Dieter Schaal gleichsam federführend eingeleitet.

Die Vorreiterrolle und der bis heute fortdauernde Erfolg seiner Bühnen- und Ausstellungsinszenierungen beruht im wesentlichen darauf, daß Schaal nachgerade auf diesem Terrain die eigene Mehrfachbegabung voll ausspielen kann. Gleichermaßen erfolgreich als Architekt, Maler, Bildhauer, Bühnenbildner, Landschaftsgestalter, Stadtvisionär, Cineast oder Literat denkend und praktizierend, hat er in den raumgreifenden szenographischen Installationen einzigartige dreidimensionale Äquivalente für seine auf Papier gezeichneten »Denk-« und »Wegräume« oder »Denkgebäude« der 1970er Jahre gefunden. Eigentlich sind in dem legendären Kompendium der *Architektonischen Situationen*, die Schaal gleichsam als Essenz seiner frühen Raumstudien im Jahr 1980 erstmals publiziert hat, im Kern bereits alle späteren Bühnen- und Ausstellungskonfigurationen angelegt.

Aus der symbiotischen Beziehung zwischen der Regielegende Ruth Berghaus und dem Raumvisionär Schaal gingen seit den frühen 1980er Jahren Bühnenbilder hervor, die Geschichte geschrieben haben. Im Zusammenwirken mit Berghaus schuf Schaal für die *Trojaner* (1983), *Wozzeck* (1984), *Orpheus* (1986), *Elektra* (1986), *Moses und Aron* (1987), *Tristan und Isolde* (1988), *Lulu* (1988), *Fierrabras* (1988), *Ariane et Barbe-Bleue* (1991) und *Nachtwache* (1993) sowie dann auch mit anderen Regisseuren für unzählige weitere Opern und Theaterstücke bis heute nachwirkende, elementare Raumsetzungen von großer Suggestivkraft. Dekonstruierte Raumkonstellationen, schräg ineinander verkeilte Ebenen, perspektivisch verdrehte Architekturen, gigantische Planetenkörper oder wie in Eis erstarrte Landschaften und endlose Tiefen des Weltraums verdichteten sich dabei zu nie gesehenen, wie traumhaft hingesagten Bildern; zu Bildern, die stets archaische Erinnerungen oder verschüttete Sehnsüchte freilegen. Schaal betrachtet sich dabei nie als Illustrator des jeweiligen szenischen Geschehens, sondern als emanzipierter szenischer Choreograph von Bildtableaus, welche das spezifische Bühnengeschehen als zusätzliche, gleichwohl verborgene Handlungsstränge kommentieren, interpretieren und gedanklich weiterspinnen.

Dies trifft gleichermaßen auch auf seine Konzepte für temporäre oder dauerhafte Ausstellungen zu. Vor jedem Einzelprojekt aus der langen Liste seiner großen oder kleineren Ausstellungen recherchiert Schaal mit beinahe wissenschaftlicher Akribie archivalische Grundlagen, historische Hintergründe und Nachwirkungen, aber auch emotionale oder psychoanalytische Implikationen der jeweiligen Ausstellungsthematik und der mit ihr verbundenen Exponate. In Arbeiten wie etwa seinen Installationen für *Berlin – Berlin* (1987) oder *Prometheus* (1998), für das Filmmuseum Berlin (2000) sowie die Gedenkstätten der ehrmaligen KZs Mittelbau-Dora (2006), Bergen-Belsen (2007) oder Esterwegen (2011) präsentiert er stets auch seine eigene Sicht der Welt, seine eigene Sicht der Dinge.

Ganz entfernt an Schinkels Umgang mit Spolien im Park von Glienicke erinnernd, betrachtet Schaal Exponate wie Fundstücke aus einer verlorenen Zeit. Diese Fundstücke versucht er einzukreisen, ihren kulturgeschichtlichen Wert und ihre Wirkung ein- und abzuschätzen, um ihnen in seinen 3D-Kartographien verborgener Beziehungen schließlich einen festen Platz zuzuweisen. So konfigurieren sich Exponate, eingefaßt von eindrücklichen architektonischen »Tableaux vivants«, zu nie zuvor gesehenen, begehbaren Traumstädten oder Traumlandschaften, die den Besucher nicht unberührt lassen. Statt dessen ermuntern sie ihn zum Betreten eines jeweils gänzlich neu aufbereiteten »Terrain vague«, bei dessen Erkundung Empathie und Anteilnahme mitunter höher angesetzt sind als kognitives Wissen. Auf diese Weise macht Schaal die Besucher seiner Ausstellungen zu Expeditionsteilnehmern, welche die »Tropen« seiner Ausstellungslandschaften auf verschlungenen Pfaden durchwandern und erleben.

»Die äußere Erscheinung der Welt, wie sie mir sinnlich gegeben ist, reicht« nach den Worten von Michael Hauskeller »für sich allein genommen nicht hin, um die atmosphärische Erfahrung verständlich zu machen. Die Welt ist für mich in ihrer Gegebenheit immer mehr als die bloße Erscheinung, ist erscheinende Welt, eben kein Traum, sondern erlebte Wirklichkeit. Dieses Mehr in der Erfahrung, das die bloße Erscheinung als Ansammlung von Sinnesdaten transzendiert, das Welthaltige daran, ist das unerläßliche Fundament atmosphärischen Spürens, und erst dadurch erlangt die Erscheinung ihre allgemeine Bedeutsamkeit.« Hauskeller verweist damit auf ein »Dazwischen« als Zustand zwischen realer und vorgestellter Welt. Denn dieses »Dazwischen« sei »entscheidend für mein Mich-Finden-in-einer Welt.«

Dieses Mich-Finden oder Mich-Wieder-Finden in der Welt dürfte eines der wichtigsten Motive der in diesem Band versammelten Rauminstallationen sein. Mit ihnen hat Schaal der »Szenographie« eine ganz spezifische neue Bedeutung zugewiesen. Denn von keinem außer ihm wird sie so eindrücklich betrieben, diese Verführung zur atmosphärischen Einverleibung »anderer« Orte, die geradezu lustvolle Verführung zu einer »anderen«, vielleicht näher an unserer eigenen Wirklichkeit liegenden Lektüre von Geschichte.

1–3. Hector Berlioz, *Les Troyens*
Oper Frankfurt, 1983
Direction: Ruth Berghaus
Conductor: Michael Gielen
Stage set: Hans Dieter Schaal
Costumes: Nina Ritter
Photos: Mara Eggert

1–3. Hector Berlioz, *Die Trojaner*
Oper Frankfurt, 1983
Regie: Ruth Berghaus
Dirigent: Michael Gielen
Bühnenbild: Hans Dieter Schaal
Kostüme: Nina Ritter
Photos: Mara Eggert

4–6. Alban Berg, *Wozzeck*
Opéra national de Paris (Opéra Garnier), 1985
Direction: Ruth Berghaus
Conductor: Christoph von Dohnanyi
Stage set: Hans Dieter Schaal
Costumes: Marie-Luise Strandt
Photos: Jacques Moatti

4–6. Alban Berg, *Wozzeck*
Opéra national de Paris (Opéra Garnier), 1985
Regie: Ruth Berghaus
Dirigent: Christoph von Dohnanyi
Bühnenbild: Hans Dieter Schaal
Kostüme: Marie-Luise Strandt
Photos: Jacques Moatti

7–9. Alban Berg, *Wozzeck*
Opéra national de Paris (Opéra Garnier), 1985
Direction: Ruth Berghaus
Conductor: Christoph von Dohnanyi
Stage set: Hans Dieter Schaal
Costumes: Marie-Luise Strandt
Photos: Jacques Moatti

7–9. Alban Berg, *Wozzeck*
Opéra national de Paris (Opéra Garnier), 1985
Regie: Ruth Berghaus
Dirigent: Christoph von Dohnanyi
Bühnenbild: Hans Dieter Schaal
Kostüme: Marie-Luise Strandt
Photos: Jacques Moatti

10–12. Hans Werner Henze, *Orpheus*
Staatsoper Wien, 1986
Direction and choreography: Ruth Berghaus
Conductor: Ulf Schirmer
Stage set: Hans Dieter Schaal
Costumes: Marie-Luise Strandt
Photos: Axel Zeininger

10–12. Hans Werner Henze, *Orpheus*
Staatsoper Wien, 1986
Regie und Choreographie: Ruth Berghaus
Dirigent: Ulf Schirmer
Bühnenbild: Hans Dieter Schaal
Kostüme: Marie-Luise Strandt
Photos: Axel Zeininger

13–15. Lars Norén, *Ephemeral Beings*
Nederlands Toneel, Gent, 1986
Direction: Guy Joosten
Stage set: Hans Dieter Schaal
Costumes: Christine Mortier
Photos: Hans Dieter Schaal

13–15. Lars Norén, *Eintagswesen*
Nederlands Toneel, Gent, 1986
Regie: Guy Joosten
Bühnenbild: Hans Dieter Schaal
Kostüme: Christine Mortier
Photos: Hans Dieter Schaal

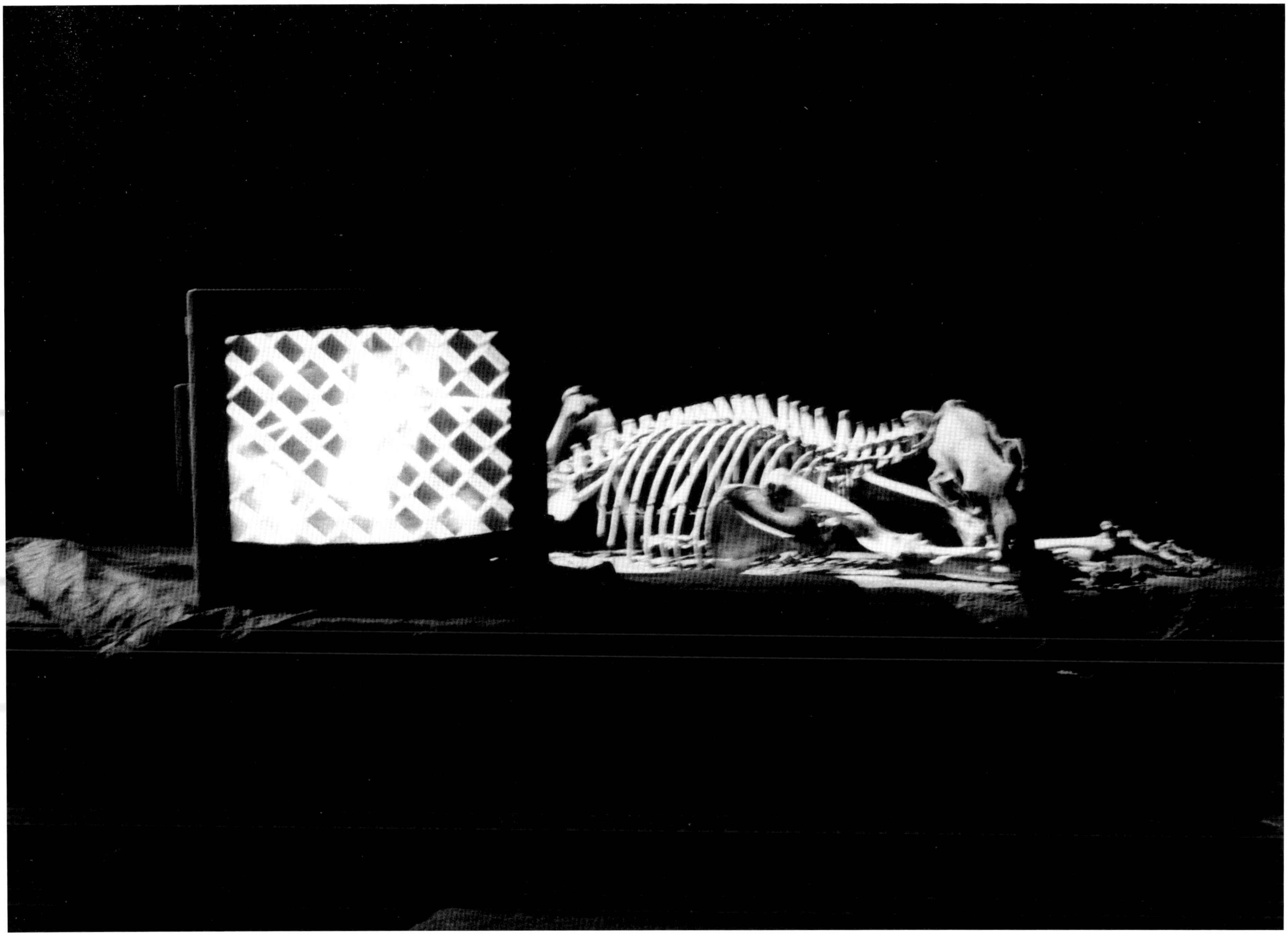

16, 17. Richard Strauss, *Elektra*
Semperoper Dresden, 1986
(Reconstruction: Opéra de Lyon, 2017)
Direction: Ruth Berghaus
Conductor: Hartmut Haenchen
Stage set: Hans Dieter Schaal
Costumes: Marie-Luise Strandt
Photos: Maria Steinfeldt

16, 17. Richard Strauss, *Elektra*
Semperoper Dresden, 1986
(Rekonstruktion: Opéra de Lyon, 2017)
Regie: Ruth Berghaus
Dirigent: Hartmut Haenchen
Bühnenbild: Hans Dieter Schaal
Kostüme: Marie-Luise Strandt
Photos: Maria Steinfeldt

TIETZ
B
im Licht

18, 19. *Berlin – Berlin*
Martin-Gropius-Bau, Berlin, 1987
Scientific direction: Gottfried Korff, Bodo Baumunk and Marie-Louise von Plessen
Exhibition architecture and presentation: Hans Dieter Schaal
Photos: Reinhard Görner

18, 19. *Berlin – Berlin*
Martin-Gropius-Bau, Berlin, 1987
Wissenschaftliche Leitung: Gottfried Korff, Bodo Baumunk und Marie-Louise von Plessen
Ausstellungsarchitektur und Inszenierung: Hans Dieter Schaal
Photos: Reinhard Görner

20–22. *Berlin – Berlin*
Martin-Gropius-Bau, Berlin, 1987
Scientific direction: Gottfried Korff, Bodo Baumunk and Marie-Louise von Plessen
Exhibition architecture and presentation: Hans Dieter Schaal
Photos: Reinhard Görner

20–22. *Berlin – Berlin*
Martin-Gropius-Bau, Berlin, 1987
Wissenschaftliche Leitung: Gottfried Korff, Bodo Baumunk und Marie-Louise von Plessen
Ausstellungsarchitektur und Inszenierung: Hans Dieter Schaal
Photos: Reinhard Görner

23–25. Arnold Schönberg, ***Moses und Aron***
Deutsche Staatsoper Berlin, 1987
Direction: Ruth Berghaus
Conductor: Friedrich Goldmann
Stage set: Hans Dieter Schaal
Costumes: Marie-Luise Strandt
Photos: Maria Steinfeldt

23–25. Arnold Schönberg, ***Moses und Aron***
Deutsche Staatsoper Berlin, 1987
Regie: Ruth Berghaus
Dirigent: Friedrich Goldmann
Bühnenbild: Hans Dieter Schaal
Kostüme: Marie-Luise Strandt
Photos: Maria Steinfeldt

26. Richard Wagner, *Tristan und Isolde*
Staatsoper Hamburg, 1988
Direction: Ruth Berghaus
Conductor: Zoltan Pesko
Stage set: Hans Dieter Schaal
Costumes: Marie-Luise Strandt
Photo: Ines Gellrich

26. Richard Wagner, *Tristan und Isolde*
Staatsoper Hamburg, 1988
Regie: Ruth Berghaus
Dirigent: Zoltan Pesko
Bühnenbild: Hans Dieter Schaal
Kostüme: Marie-Luise Strandt
Photo: Ines Gellrich

27. Paul Dukas, ***Ariane et Barbe-Bleue***
Théâtre du Châtelet, Paris, 1991
Direction: Ruth Berghaus
Conductor: Eliahu Imbal
Stage set: Hans Dieter Schaal
Costumes: Marie-Luise Strandt
Photo: Jacques Moatti

27. Paul Dukas, ***Ariane et Barbe-Bleue***
Théâtre du Châtelet, Paris, 1991
Regie: Ruth Berghaus
Dirigent: Eliahu Imbal
Bühnenbild: Hans Dieter Schaal
Kostüme: Marie-Luise Strandt
Photo: Jacques Moatti

28, 29. Richard Strauss, *Elektra*
Opernhaus Zürich, 1991
Direction: Ruth Berghaus
Conductor: Ralf Weikert
Stage set: Hans Dieter Schaal
Costumes: Marie-Luise Strandt
Photos: Hans Dieter Schaal

28, 29. Richard Strauss, *Elektra*
Opernhaus Zürich, 1991
Regie: Ruth Berghaus
Dirigent: Ralf Weikert
Bühnenbild: Hans Dieter Schaal
Kostüme: Marie-Luise Strandt
Photos: Hans Dieter Schaal

30–32. **Jörg Herchet, *Nachtwache***
Oper Leipzig, 1993, debut performance
Direction: Ruth Berghaus
Conductor: Lothar Zagrosek
Stage set: Hans Dieter Schaal
Costumes: Marie-Luise Strandt
Photos: Peter Horn

30–32. **Jörg Herchet, *Nachtwache***
Oper Leipzig, 1993, Uraufführung
Regie: Ruth Berghaus
Dirigent: Lothar Zagrosek
Bühnenbild: Hans Dieter Schaal
Kostüme: Marie-Luise Strandt
Photos: Peter Horn

33, 34. *1200 Jahre Frankfurt am Main*
Bockenheimer Depot, Frankfurt am Main, 1994
Scientific direction: Lothar Gall
Exhibition architecture and presentation: Hans Dieter Schaal
Photos: Peter Horn

33, 34. *1200 Jahre Frankfurt am Main*
Bockenheimer Depot, Frankfurt am Main, 1994
Wissenschaftliche Leitung: Lothar Gall
Ausstellungsarchitektur und Inszenierung: Hans Dieter Schaal
Photos: Peter Horn

35, 36. *Kino – Movie – Cinema*
Martin-Gropius-Bau, Berlin, 1995
Scientific direction: Hans Helmut Prinzler, Wolfgang Jacobsen and Werner Sudendorf
Exhibition architecture and presentation: Hans Dieter Schaal
Photos: Reinhard Görner

35, 36. *Kino – Movie – Cinema*
Martin-Gropius-Bau, Berlin, 1995
Wissenschaftliche Leitung: Hans Helmut Prinzler, Wolfgang Jacobsen und Werner Sudendorf
Ausstellungsarchitektur und Inszenierung: Hans Dieter Schaal
Photos: Reinhard Görner

37–39. ***Kino – Movie – Cinema***
Martin-Gropius-Bau, Berlin, 1995
Scientific direction: Hans Helmut Prinzler, Wolfgang Jacobsen and Werner Sudendorf
Exhibition architecture and presentation: Hans Dieter Schaal
Photos: Reinhard Görner

37–39. ***Kino – Movie – Cinema***
Martin-Gropius-Bau, Berlin, 1995
Wissenschaftliche Leitung: Hans Helmut Prinzler, Wolfgang Jacobsen und Werner Sudendorf
Ausstellungsarchitektur und Inszenierung: Hans Dieter Schaal
Photos: Reinhard Görner

40. Claude Debussy, ***The Fall of the House of Usher***
Oper Stuttgart, 1996
Direction: Christoph Nel
Conductor: Bernhard Kontarsky
Stage set: Hans Dieter Schaal
Costumes: Ilse Welter
Photo: Oper Stuttgart

40. Claude Debussy, ***Der Fall des Hauses Usher***
Oper Stuttgart, 1996
Regie: Christoph Nel
Dirigent: Bernhard Kontarsky
Bühnenbild: Hans Dieter Schaal
Kostüme: Ilse Welter
Photo: Oper Stuttgart

41–43. Wolfgang Amadeus Mozart, *The Magic Flute*
Hessisches Staatstheater Wiesbaden, 1996
Direction: Dominik Neuner
Conductor: Toshiyuki Kamioka
Stage set: Hans Dieter Schaal
Costumes: Ute Frühling
Photos: Bettina Müller

41–43. Wolfgang Amadeus Mozart, *Die Zauberflöte*
Hessisches Staatstheater Wiesbaden, 1996
Regie: Dominik Neuner
Dirigent: Toshiyuki Kamioka
Bühnenbild: Hans Dieter Schaal
Kostüme: Ute Frühling
Photos: Bettina Müller

WOHLSTAND
FREIHEIT
FÜR ALLE
FREIES
VEREINIGUNGS-
RECHT

44, 45. *1848 – Aufbruch zur Freiheit*
Schirn Kunsthalle, Frankfurt am Main, 1996
Scientific direction: Lothar Gall
Exhibition architecture and presentation: Hans Dieter Schaal
Exhibition graphics: Alex Koerfer
Photos: Peter Horn

44, 45. *1848 – Aufbruch zur Freiheit*
Schirn Kunsthalle, Frankfurt am Main, 1996
Wissenschaftliche Leitung: Lothar Gall
Ausstellungsarchitektur und Inszenierung: Hans Dieter Schaal
Ausstellungsgraphik: Alex Koerfer
Photos: Peter Horn

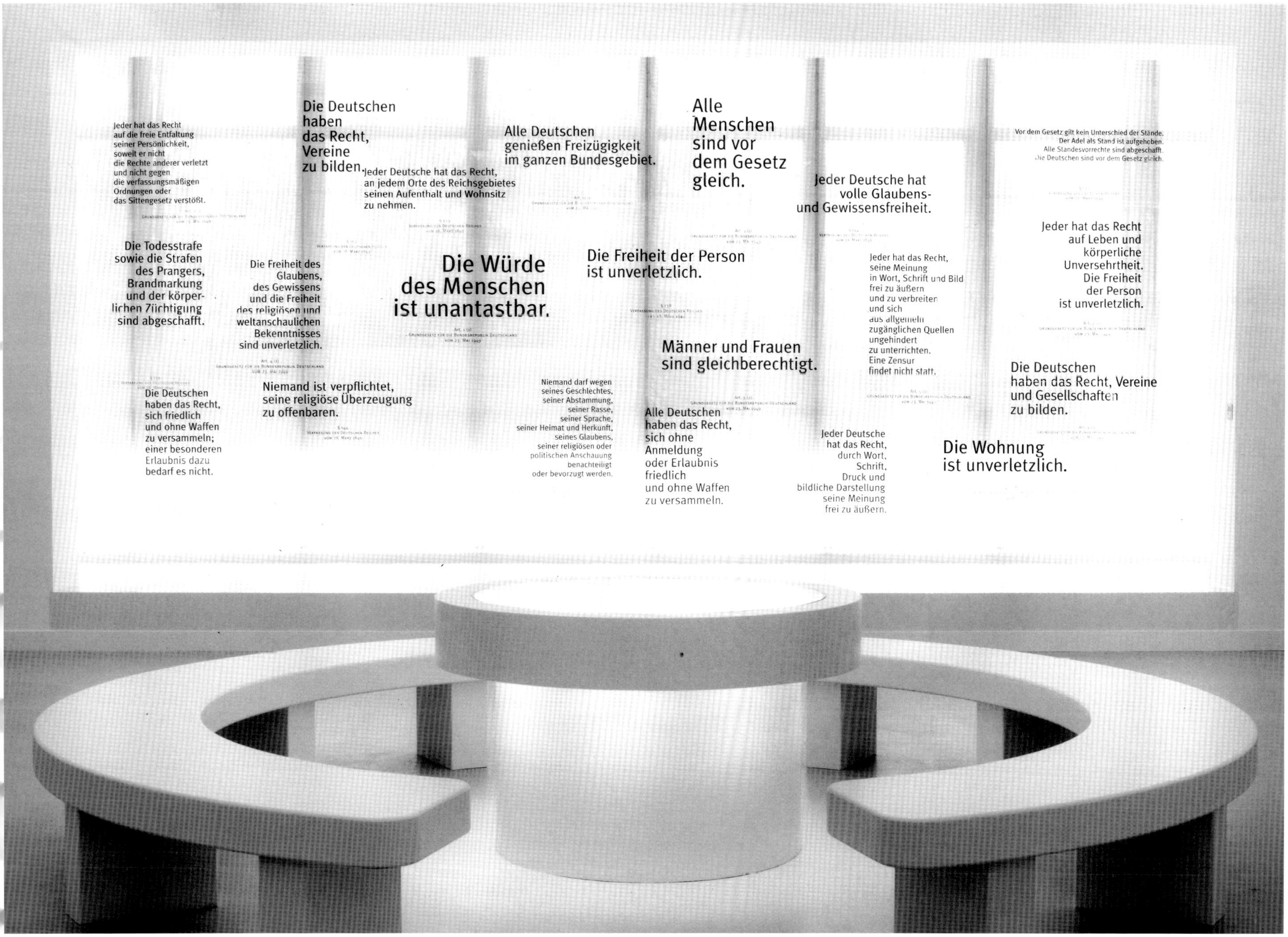

46–48. *Poetik der Türen*
Kultur Bahnhof Eller, Düsseldorf, 1997
Ausstellung mit eigenen Arbeiten

46–48. *Poetik der Türen*
Kultur Bahnhof Eller, Düsseldorf, 1997
Exhibition with own works

49, 50. Pietro Mascagni, *Cavalleria Rusticana, and* Ruggiero Leoncavallo, *Bajazzo*
Bremer Theater, 1998
Direction: Dominik Neuner
Conductor: Günter Neuhold
Stage set: Hans Dieter Schaal
Costumes: Swetlana Zwetkowa
Photos: Bremer Theater

49, 50. Pietro Mascagni, *Cavalleria Rusticana,* und Ruggiero Leoncavallo, *Bajazzo*
Bremer Theater, 1998
Regie: Dominik Neuner
Dirigent: Günter Neuhold
Bühnenbild: Hans Dieter Schaal
Kostüme: Swetlana Zwetkowa
Photos: Bremer Theater

51, 52. Hans Werner Henze, *Boulevard Solitude*
Oper Frankfurt, 1998
Direction: Nicolas Brieger
Conductor: Bernhard Kontarsky
Stage set: Hans Dieter Schaal
Costumes: Jorge Jara
Photos: Oper Frankfurt

51, 52. Hans Werner Henze, *Boulevard Solitude*
Oper Frankfurt, 1998
Regie: Nicolas Brieger
Dirigent: Bernhard Kontarsky
Bühnenbild: Hans Dieter Schaal
Kostüme: Jorge Jara
Photos: Oper Frankfurt

Selbstschöpfung
chkeit

53, 54. *Prometheus – Menschen, Bilder, Visionen*
Blower hall of the Völklinger Hütte, 1998
Scientific direction: Rosmarie Beier-de Haan
Exhibition architecture and presentation: Hans Dieter Schaal
Photos: Reinhard Görner

53, 54. *Prometheus – Menschen, Bilder, Visionen*
Gebläsehalle der Völklinger Hütte, 1998
Wissenschaftliche Leitung: Rosmarie Beier-de Haan
Ausstellungsarchitektur und Inszenierung: Hans Dieter Schaal
Photos: Reinhard Görner

55, 56. ***Prometheus – Menschen, Bilder, Visionen***
Blower hall of the Völklinger Hütte, 1998
Scientific direction: Rosmarie Beier-de Haan
Exhibition architecture and presentation: Hans Dieter Schaal
Photos: Reinhard Görner

55, 56. ***Prometheus – Menschen, Bilder, Visionen***
Gebläsehalle der Völklinger Hütte, 1998
Wissenschaftliche Leitung: Rosmarie Beier-de Haan
Ausstellungsarchitektur und Inszenierung: Hans Dieter Schaal
Photos: Reinhard Görner

57–59. Ferruccio Busoni, *Doktor Faust*
Staatstheater Nürnberg, 1998
Direction: Jürgen Tamchina
Stage set: Hans Dieter Schaal
Costumes: Beate Tamchina
Photos: Staatstheater Nürnberg

57–59. Ferruccio Busoni, *Doktor Faust*
Staatstheater Nürnberg, 1998
Regie: Jürgen Tamchina
Bühnenbild: Hans Dieter Schaal
Kostüme: Beate Tamchina
Photos: Staatstheater Nürnberg

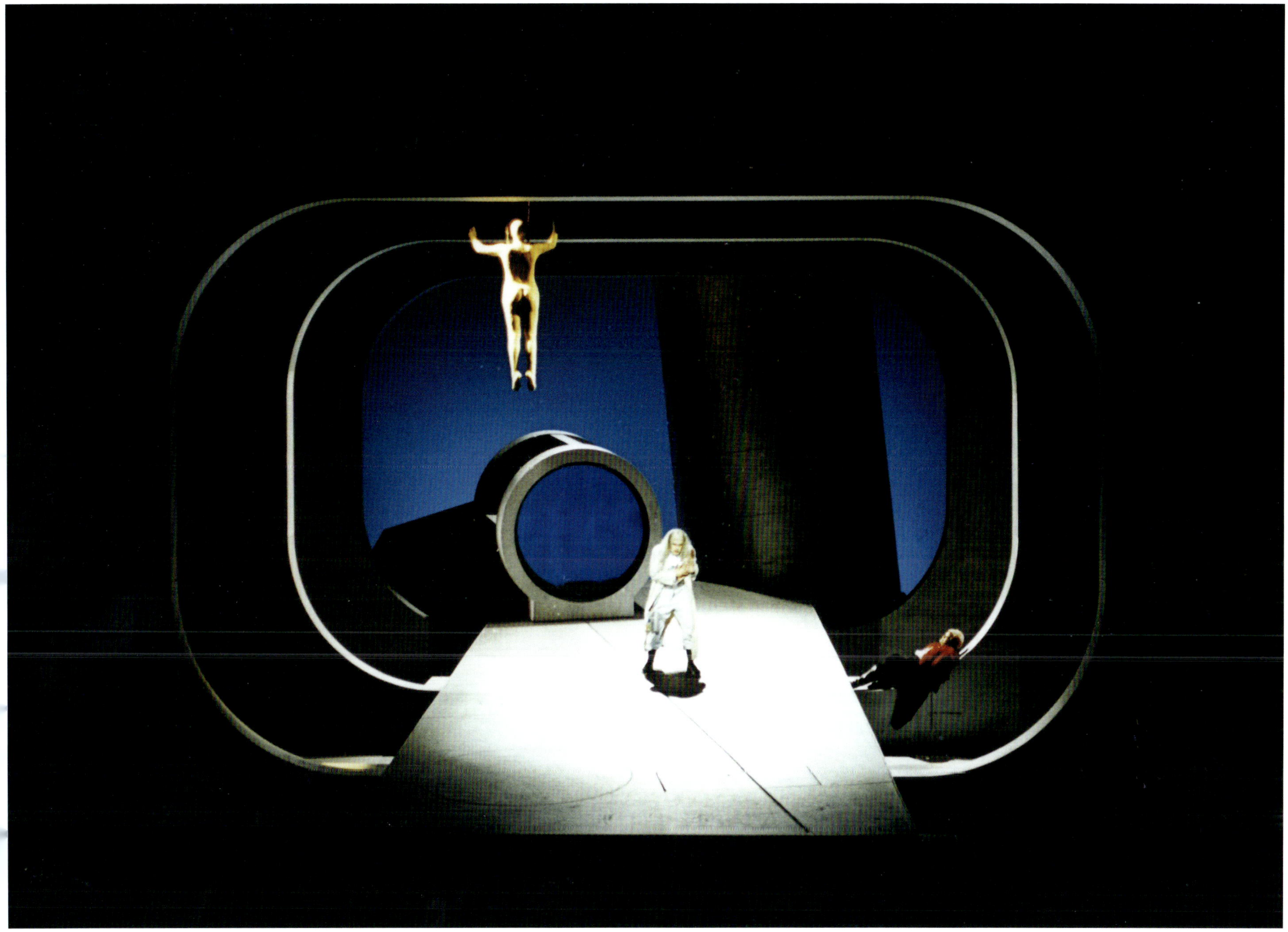

60, 61. Wolfgang Amadeus Mozart,
The Abduction from the Seraglio
Theater Lübeck, 1999
Direction: Jürgen Tamchina
Conductor. Rüdiger Bohn
Stage set: Hans Dieter Schaal
Costumes: Beate Tamchina
Photos: Hans Dieter Schaal

60, 61. Wolfgang Amadeus Mozart,
Die Entführung aus dem Serail
Theater Lübeck, 1999
Regie: Jürgen Tamchina
Dirigent: Rüdiger Bohn
Bühnenbild: Hans Dieter Schaal
Kostüme: Beate Tamchina
Photos: Hans Dieter Schaal

62–65. Filmmuseum Berlin
Sony Center, Berlin, 2000
Scientific direction: Hans Helmut Prinzler, Wolfgang Jacobsen and Werner Sudendorf
Exhibition architecture and presentation: Hans Dieter Schaal
Photos: Reinhard Görner

62–65. Filmmuseum Berlin
Sony Center, Berlin, 2000
Wissenschaftliche Leitung: Hans Helmut Prinzler, Wolfgang Jacobsen und Werner Sudendorf
Ausstellungsarchitektur und Inszenierung: Hans Dieter Schaal
Photos: Reinhard Görner

66–68. Gabriel Urbain Fauré, Pénélope
Opernhaus Chemnitz, 2002
Direction and choreography: Arila Siegert
Conductor: Fabrice Bollon
Stage set: Hans Dieter Schaal
Costumes: Marie-Luise Strandt
Photos: Maria Steinfeldt

66–68. Gabriel Urbain Fauré, Pénélope
Opernhaus Chemnitz, 2002
Regie und Choreographie: Arila Siegert
Dirigent: Fabrice Bollon
Bühnenbild: Hans Dieter Schaal
Kostüme: Marie-Luise Strandt
Photos: Maria Steinfeldt

69, 70. Olivier Messiaen, *Saint François d'Assise*
San Francisco Opera, 2002
Direction: Nicolas Brieger
Conductor: Donald Runnicles
Stage set: Hans Dieter Schaal
Costumes: Andrea Schmidt-Futterer
Photos: San Francisco Opera

69, 70. Olivier Messiaen, *Saint François d'Assise*
San Francisco Opera, 2002
Regie: Nicolas Brieger
Dirigent: Donald Runnicles
Bühnenbild: Hans Dieter Schaal
Kostüme: Andrea Schmidt-Futterer
Photos: San Francisco Opera

71–73. Hans Werner Henze, *Das verratene Meer*
Oper Frankfurt, 2002
Direction: Nicolas Brieger
Conductor: Bernhard Kontarsky
Stage set: Hans Dieter Schaal
Costumes: Margit Koppendorfer
Photos: Thilo Beu

71–73. Hans Werner Henze, *Das verratene Meer*
Oper Frankfurt, 2002
Regie: Nicolas Brieger
Dirigent: Bernhard Kontarsky
Bühnenbild: Hans Dieter Schaal
Kostüme: Margit Koppendorfer
Photos: Thilo Beu

74–76. Giacomo Rossini, ***The Barber of Seville***
San Francisco Opera, 2003
Direction: Johannes Schaaf
Conductor: Stefan Soltesz
Stage set: Hans Dieter Schaal
Costumes: Yan Tax
Photos: Hans Dieter Schaal

74–76. Giacomo Rossini, ***Der Barbier von Sevilla***
San Francisco Opera, 2003
Regie: Johannes Schaaf
Dirigent: Stefan Soltesz
Bühnenbild: Hans Dieter Schaal
Kostüme: Yan Tax
Photos: Hans Dieter Schaal

77–79. *Das Rätsel der Kelten*
Schirn Kunsthalle, Frankfurt am Main, 2003
Exhibition architecture and presentation: Hans Dieter Schaal
Photos: Melanie Brugger

77–79. *Das Rätsel der Kelten*
Schirn Kunsthalle, Frankfurt am Main, 2003
Ausstellungsarchitektur und Inszenierung: Hans Dieter Schaal
Photos: Melanie Brugger

80–82. Pyotr Ilyich Tchaikovsky, *Eugen Onegin*
Opernhaus Chemnitz, 2003
Direction: Arila Siegert
Conductor: Niksa Bareza
Stage set: Hans Dieter Schaal
Costumes: Marie-Luise Strandt
Photos: Maria Steinfeldt

80–82. Pjotr Iljitsch Tschaikowski, *Eugen Onegin*
Opernhaus Chemnitz, 2003
Regie: Arila Siegert
Dirigent: Niksa Bareza
Bühnenbild: Hans Dieter Schaal
Kostüme: Marie-Luise Strandt
Photos: Maria Steinfeldt

83–85. Carl Maria von Weber, ***The Freeshooter***
Opernhaus Chemnitz, 2003
Direction: Arila Siegert
Conductor: Niksa Bareza
Stage set: Hans Dieter Schaal
Costumes: Marie-Luise Strandt
Photos: Maria Steinfeldt

83–85. Carl Maria von Weber, ***Der Freischütz***
Opernhaus Chemnitz, 2003
Regie: Arila Siegert
Dirigent: Niksa Bareza
Bühnenbild: Hans Dieter Schaal
Kostüme: Marie-Luise Strandt
Photos: Maria Steinfeldt

86, 87. Alban Berg, *Wozzeck*
Aalto-Musiktheater, Essen, 2004
Direction: Johannes Schaaf
Conductor: Stefan Soltesz
Stage set: Hans Dieter Schaal
Costumes: Marie-Luise Strandt
Photos: Bernd Schmidt

86, 87. Alban Berg, *Wozzeck*
Aalto-Musiktheater, Essen, 2004
Regie: Johannes Schaaf
Dirigent: Stefan Soltesz
Bühnenbild: Hans Dieter Schaal
Kostüme: Marie-Luise Strandt
Photos: Bernd Schmidt

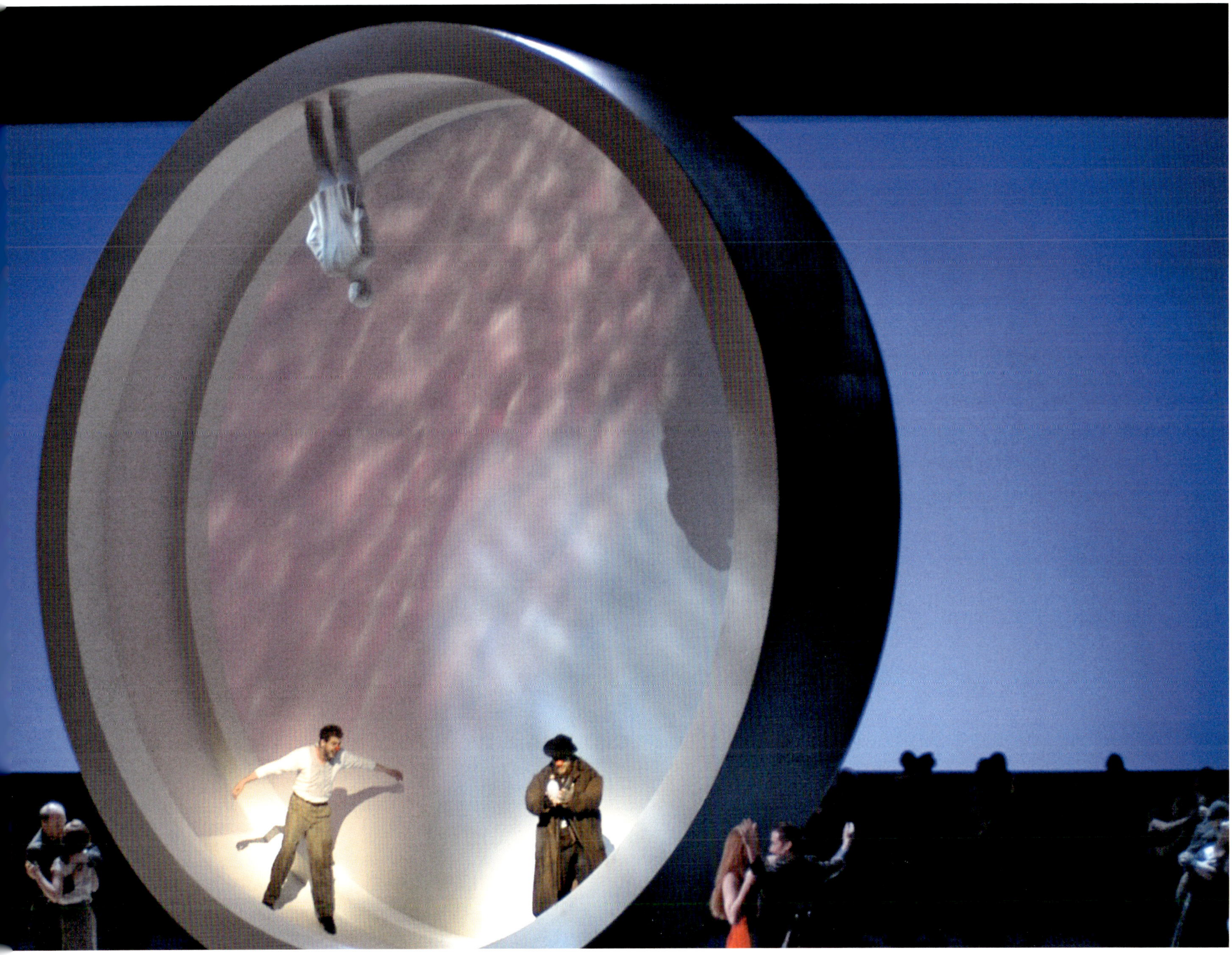

88, 89. Wolfgang Amadeus Mozart, *The Magic Flute*
Theater Osnabrück and Vanemuine, Tartu, 2005
Direction: Arila Siegert
Conductors: Marius Stieghorst and Hendrik Vestmann
Stage set: Hans Dieter Schaal
Costumes: Marie-Luise Strandt
Photos: Hans Dieter Schaal

88, 89. Wolfgang Amadeus Mozart, *Die Zauberflöte*
Theater Osnabrück und Vanemuine, Tartu, 2005
Regie: Arila Siegert
Dirigenten: Marius Stieghorst und Hendrik Vestmann
Bühnenbild: Hans Dieter Schaal
Kostüme: Marie-Luise Strandt
Photos: Hans Dieter Schaal

90–92. Fernsehmuseum Berlin
Sony Center, Berlin, 2005
Scientific direction: Peter Paul Kubitz
Exhibition architecture and presentation: Hans Dieter Schaal
Photos: Hillert Ibbeken

90–92. Fernsehmuseum Berlin
Sony Center, Berlin, 2005
Wissenschaftliche Leitung: Peter Paul Kubitz
Ausstellungsarchitektur und Inszenierung: Hans Dieter Schaal
Photos: Hillert Ibbeken

1967 - 1984

93–95. Jacques Offenbach, ***The Tales of Hoffmann***
Opernhaus Graz, 2006
Direction: Tatjana Gürbaca
Conductor: Wolfgang Bosic
Stage set: Hans Dieter Schaal
Costumes: Michaela Meyer-Michnay
Photos: Opernhaus Graz

93–95. Jacques Offenbach, ***Hoffmanns Erzählungen***
Opernhaus Graz, 2006
Regie: Tatjana Gürbaca
Dirigent: Wolfgang Bosic
Bühnenbild: Hans Dieter Schaal
Kostüme: Michaela Meyer-Michnay
Photos: Opernhaus Graz

96–98. *Heimat und Exil*
Jüdisches Museum Berlin, 2006
Scientific direction: Margret Kampmeyer, Cilly Kugelmann and Jürgen Reiche
Exhibition architecture and presentation: Hans Dieter Schaal
Photos: Hans Dieter Schaal

96–98. *Heimat und Exil*
Jüdisches Museum Berlin, 2006
Wissenschaftliche Leitung: Margret Kampmeyer, Cilly Kugelmann und Jürgen Reiche
Ausstellungs-Architektur und Inszenierung: Hans Dieter Schaal
Photos: Hans Dieter Schaal

99–101. Erich Wolfgang Korngold, ***The Dead City***
Grand Théâtre de Genève, 2006
Direction: Nicolas Brieger
Conductor: Armin Jordan
Stage set: Hans Dieter Schaal
Costumes: Andrea Schmidt-Futterer
Photos: Hans Dieter Schaal

99–101. Erich Wolfgang Korngold, ***Die tote Stadt***
Grand Théâtre de Genève, 2006
Regie: Nicolas Brieger
Dirigent: Armin Jordan
Bühnenbild: Hans Dieter Schaal
Kostüme: Andrea Schmidt-Futterer
Photos: Hans Dieter Schaal

102–104. Sergei Prokofiev, *Cinderella*
Bolshoi Theatre, Moskow, 2006
Choreography: Yuri Possokhov
Conductor: Alexander Vedernikov
Stage set: Hans Dieter Schaal
Costumes: Sandra Woodall
Photos: Hans Dieter Schaal

102–104. Sergej Prokofjew, *Cinderella*
Bolshoi-Theater, Moskau, 2006
Choreographie: Yuri Prossokow
Dirigent: Alexander Vedernikow
Bühnenbild: Hans Dieter Schaal
Kostüme: Sandra Woodall
Photos: Hans Dieter Schaal

Guest perfomances / Gastspiele:
Royal Opera House, London; John F. Kennedy Center for the Performing Arts, Washington, D.C., 2007

105–107. Dmitri Shostakovich, *The Nose*
Aalto-Musiktheater, Essen, 2006
Direction: Johannes Schaaf
Conductor: Stefan Soltesz
Stage set: Hans Dieter Schaal
Costumes: René Listerdal
Photos: Berd Schmidt

105–107. Dmitri Schostakowitsch, *Die Nase*
Aalto-Musiktheater, Essen, 2006
Regie: Johannes Schaaf
Dirigent: Stefan Soltesz
Bühnenbild: Hans Dieter Schaal
Kostüme: René Listerdal
Photos: Berd Schmidt

108, 109. Pyotr Ilyich Tchaikovsky, *Pique Dame*
Wuppertaler Bühnen, 2006
Stage director: Dominik Neuner
Conductor: Toshiyuki Kamioka
Stage set: Hans Dieter Schaal
Costumes: Marie-Luise Strandt
Photos: Hans Dieter Schaal

108, 109. Pjotr Iljitsch Tschaikowski, *Pique Dame*
Wuppertaler Bühnen, 2006
Regie: Dominik Neuner
Dirigent: Toshiyuki Kamioka
Bühnenbild: Hans Dieter Schaal
Kostüme: Marie-Luise Strandt
Photos: Hans Dieter Schaal

110, 111. Franz Lehár, *The Merry Widow*
Theater Görlitz, 2006
Direction and choreography: Arila Siegert
Conductor: Milos Krejcí
Stage set: Hans Dieter Schaal
Costumes: Marie-Luise Strandt
Photos: Maria Steinfeldt

110, 111. Franz Lehár, *Die lustige Witwe*
Theater Görlitz, 2006
Regie und Choreographie: Arila Siegert
Dirigent: Milos Krejcí
Bühnenbild: Hans Dieter Schaal
Kostüme: Marie-Luise Strandt
Photos: Maria Steinfeldt

112, 113. Leoš Janáček, *The Makropoulos Affair*
Landestheater Neustrelitz, 2007
Direction: Arila Siegert
Conductor: Stefan Malzew
Stage set: Hans Dieter Schaal
Costumes: Marie-Luise Strandt
Photos: Maria Steinfeldt

112, 113. Leoš Janáček, *Die Sache Makropulos*
Landestheater Neustrelitz, 2007
Regie: Arila Siegert
Dirigent: Stefan Malzew
Bühnenbild: Hans Dieter Schaal
Kostüme: Marie-Luise Strandt
Photos: Maria Steinfeldt

114. Eugen d'Albert, *The Lowlands*
Deutsche Oper Berlin, 2007
Direction: Roland Schwab
Conductor: Yves Abel
Stage set: Hans Dieter Schaal
Costumes: René Listerdal
Photo: Marcus Lieberenz

114. Eugen d'Albert, *Tiefland*
Deutsche Oper Berlin, 2007
Regie: Roland Schwab
Dirigent: Yves Abel
Bühnenbild: Hans Dieter Schaal
Kostüme: René Listerdal
Photo: Marcus Lieberenz

115, 116. Domenico Scarlatti, *La Giuditta*
Staatstheater Mainz, 2007
Direction: Arila Siegert
Conductor: Clemens Heil
Stage set: Hans Dieter Schaal
Costumes: Susanne Maier-Staufen
Photos: Hans Dieter Schaal

115, 116. Domenico Scarlatti, *La Giuditta*
Staatstheater Mainz, 2007
Regie: Arila Siegert
Dirigent: Clemens Heil
Bühnenbild: Hans Dieter Schaal
Kostüme: Susanne Maier-Staufen
Photos: Hans Dieter Schaal

117, 118. Richard Wagner, *The Flying Dutchman*
Landestheater Neustrelitz, 2007
Direction: Arila Siegert
Conductor: Stefan Malzew
Stage set: Hans Dieter Schaal
Costumes: Marie-Luise Strandt
Photos: Maria Steinfeldt

117, 118. Richard Wagner, *Der fliegende Holländer*
Landestheater Neustrelitz, 2007
Regie: Arila Siegert
Dirigent: Stefan Malzew
Bühnenbild: Hans Dieter Schaal
Kostüme: Marie-Luise Strandt
Photos: Maria Steinfeldt

119. Johann Strauss, *Das Spitzentuch der Königin*
Staatsoperette Dresden, 2007
Direction and choreography: Arila Siegert
Conductor: Ernst Theis
Stage set: Hans Dieter Schaal
Costumes: Marie-Luise Strandt
Photo: Hans Dieter Schaal

120. Ludwig van Beethoven, *Fidelio*
Opernhaus Kiel, 2007
Direction: Dominik Neuner
Conductor: Georg Fritzsch
Stage set: Hans Dieter Schaal
Costumes: Julia Debus
Photo: Hans Dieter Schaal

119. Johann Strauss, *Das Spitzentuch der Königin*
Staatsoperette Dresden, 2007
Regie und Choreographie: Arila Siegert
Dirigent: Ernst Theis
Bühnenbild: Hans Dieter Schaal
Kostüme: Marie-Luise Strandt
Photo: Hans Dieter Schaal

120. Ludwig van Beethoven, *Fidelio*
Opernhaus Kiel, 2007
Regie: Dominik Neuner
Dirigent: Georg Fritzsch
Bühnenbild: Hans Dieter Schaal
Kostüme: Julia Debus
Photo: Hans Dieter Schaal

121. Bohuslav Martinu, *The Greek Passion*
Opernhaus Zürich, 2008
Direction: Nicolas Brieger
Conductor: Eivind Gullberg Jensen
Stage set: Hans Dieter Schaal
Costumes: Jorge Jara
Photo: Hans Dieter Schaal

122. Pyotr Ilyich Tchaikovsky, *Pique Dame*
Theater Bonn, Opernhaus, 2008
Direction: Johannes Schaaf
Conductor: Roman Kofman
Stage set: Hans Dieter Schaal
Costumes: René Listerdal
Photo: Hans Dieter Schaal

121. Bohuslav Martinu, *The Greek Passion*
Opernhaus Zürich, 2008
Regie: Nicolas Brieger
Dirigent: Eivind Gullberg Jensen
Bühnenbild: Hans Dieter Schaal
Kostüme: Jorge Jara
Photo: Hans Dieter Schaal

122. Pjotr Iljitsch Tschaikowski, *Pique Dame*
Theater Bonn, Opernhaus, 2008
Regie: Johannes Schaaf
Dirigent: Roman Kofman
Bühnenbild: Hans Dieter Schaal
Kostüme: René Listerdal
Photo: Hans Dieter Schaal

123. Henry Purcell, ***Dido and Aeneas***
Staatstheater Mainz, 2008
Direction: Arila Siegert
Conductor: Michael Schneider
Stage set: Hans Dieter Schaal
Costumes: Susanne Maier-Staufen
Photo: Hans Dieter Schaal

124. Wolfgang Amadeus Mozart, ***The Marriage of Figaro***
Staatstheater Mainz, 2009
Direction: Arila Siegert
Conductor: Thomas Dorsch
Stage set: Hans Dieter Schaal
Costumes: Susanne Maier-Staufen
Photo: Hans Dieter Schaal

123. Henry Purcell, ***Dido und Aeneas***
Staatstheater Mainz, 2008
Regie: Arila Siegert
Dirigent: Michael Schneider
Bühnenbild: Hans Dieter Schaal
Kostüme: Susanne Maier-Staufen
Photo: Hans Dieter Schaal

124. Wolfgang Amadeus Mozart, ***Die Hochzeit des Figaro***
Staatstheater Mainz, 2009
Regie: Arila Siegert
Dirigent: Thomas Dorsch
Bühnenbild: Hans Dieter Schaal
Kostüme: Susanne Maier-Staufen
Photo: Hans Dieter Schaal

125. Carlisle Floyd, *The Passion of Jonathan Wade*
Landestheater Salzburg, 2010
Direction: Arila Siegert
Conductor: Adrian Kelly
Stage set: Hans Dieter Schaal
Costumes: Marie-Luise Strandt
Photo: Hans Dieter Schaal

126. Giacomo Puccini, *Turandot*
Staatstheater Saarbrücken, 2010
Direction: Dominik Neuner
Conductor: Toshiyuki Kamioka
Stage set: Hans Dieter Schaal
Costumes: Marie-Luise Strand
Photo: Hans Dieter Schaal

125. Carlisle Floyd, *The Passion of Jonathan Wade*
Landestheater Salzburg, 2010
Regie: Arila Siegert
Dirigent: Adrian Kelly
Bühnenbild: Hans Dieter Schaal
Kostüme: Marie-Luise Strandt
Photo: Hans Dieter Schaal

126. Giacomo Puccini, *Turandot*
Staatstheater Saarbrücken, 2010
Regie: Dominik Neuner
Dirigent: Toshiyuki Kamioka
Bühnenbild: Hans Dieter Schaal
Kostüme: Marie-Luise Strand
Photo: Hans Dieter Schaal

127–129. Giant wine barrel
Festung Königstein, 2011
Artistic installation: Hans Dieter Schaal
Photos: Melanie Brugger and Armin Teufel

127–129. Riesenweinfaß
Festung Königstein, 2011
Künstlerische Installation: Hans Dieter Schaal
Photos: Melanie Brugger und Armin Teufel

130, 131. *Hans Dieter Schaal – Denkgebäude mit Mond* (»Hans Dieter Schaal, buildings of thought with moon«)
Museum Ulm, 2012
Photos: Melanie Brugger and Armin Teufel

130, 131. *Hans Dieter Schaal – Denkgebäude mit Mond*
Museum Ulm, 2012
Photos: Melanie Brugger und Armin Teufel

132, 133. Leoš Janáček, *Jenufa*
Opernhaus Kiel, 2013
Direction: Arila Siegert
Conductor: Leo Siberski
Stage set: Hans Dieter Schaal
Costumes: Marie-Luise Strandt
Photos: Hans Dieter Schaal

132, 133. Leoš Janáček, *Jenufa*
Opernhaus Kiel, 2013
Regie: Arila Siegert
Dirigent: Leo Siberski
Bühnenbild: Hans Dieter Schaal
Kostüme: Marie-Luise Strandt
Photos: Hans Dieter Schaal

134, 135. ***Auf nackter Haut*** **(»On bare skin«)**
Haus der Geschichte Baden-Württemberg, Stuttgart, 2015
Scientific direction: Paula Lutum-Lenger and Immo Wagner-Douglas
Exhibition architecture and presentation: Hans Dieter Schaal
Photos: Melanie Brugger and Armin Teufel

134, 135. ***Auf nackter Haut***
Haus der Geschichte Baden-Württemberg, Stuttgart, 2015
Wissenschaftliche Leitung: Paula Lutum-Lenger und Immo Wagner-Douglas
Ausstellungsarchitektur und Inszenierung: Hans Dieter Schaal
Photos: Melanie Brugger und Armin Teufel

136, 137. *In Lapide Regis – On the King's Stone. 800 Years of Life at Königstein Fortress*
Festung Königstein, 2015
Scientific direction: Angelika Taube
Exhibition architecture: Hans Dieter Schaal
Figures and dioramas: m.o.l.i.t.o.r. GmbH
Photos: Bernd Walther

136, 137. *In Lapide Regis – Auf dem Stein des Königs. 800 Jahre Leben auf der Festung Königstein*
Festung Königstein, 2015
Wissenschaftliche Leitung: Angelika Taube
Ausstellungsarchitektur: Hans Dieter Schaal
Figuren und Dioramen: m.o.l.i.t.o.r. GmbH
Photos: Bernd Walther

138–140. *In Lapide Regis – On the King's Stone. 800 Years of Life at Königstein Fortress*
Festung Königstein, 2015
Scientific direction: Angelika Taube
Exhibition architecture: Hans Dieter Schaal
Figures and dioramas: m.o.l.i.t.o.r. GmbH
Photos: Bernd Walther

138–140. *In Lapide Regis – Auf dem Stein des Königs. 800 Jahre Leben auf der Festung Königstein*
Festung Königstein, 2015
Wissenschaftliche Leitung: Angelika Taube
Ausstellungsarchitektur: Hans Dieter Schaal
Figuren und Dioramen: m.o.l.i.t.o.r. GmbH
Photos: Bernd Walther

Hans Dieter Schaal

On my works

Looking back over the works I have created over more than 32 years, and over the photographs selected for this book, it appears to me – as so often before – that the stage sets and exhibition designs are really more what I call »scenic architecture« and »staged-scene spaces«. I have been able to express my enthusiasm for this kind of work in my designs, drawings, sketches, and models, but rarely to actually implement the work in real architecture or landscape designs. The actual day-today life of cities is dominated by purely functional solutions – largely for reasons of cost. The only places where »staged-scene« spaces and images are permitted are the shopping precincts, the department stores, and the malls, where they serve a clear functional intention. Shop owners and mall operators have no desire to shock passers-by or to give them a powerful artistic experience, merely to turn them into happy, enthusiastic buyers. These »staged scenes« serve as a lure, as a means of seduction.

The old yearnings for romanticism and fairytale delights are permitted to emerge and blossom at certain times of the year – around Christmas, for instance, when the shopping trip becomes a euphoric family experience. For the space of a few weeks – or even for months – streets, façades, and the interiors of department stores are given a sparkling, choreographed coating, using scenes are taken from ancient Christian traditions, from tales, and from films. Christmas trees with an icing-sugar covering of snow, Santas with sleighs filled with presents, romantic crib scenes, artificial snow and icicles, tinsel angels, and live sheep and donkeys are used in an effort to create an atmosphere far removed from the present day.

At fairs, in pleasure parks, variety venues, and in the circus big top, this magic – albeit without the Christian aspect – is a part of everyday life. The boundaries between this world and the world of theatre, opera, and shows are fluid. The phenomenal technology we have today can transform whole stadiums into audio and light domes, with the effects fully experienced by hundreds of thousands of attendees.

In centuries past, aristocrats and wealthy citizens would visibly display their wealth and social status – using staged scenes to do so. They would build elegantly decorated villas with sophisticated landscaped gardens and parks, and decorate the façades of their houses with the family coat of arms, with ornaments, with pillars, with sculptures and with stone vases. They would also celebrate lavish banquets, featuring scenes crafted in food, concerts, ballet, living theatrical tableaux, and, after dark, firework displays.

These activities were, of course, efforts to compete with prominent royal efforts in the same field. Versailles remained, for many centuries, the shining, gilded example. And the gardens by Le Nôtre showed the civilised world how nature should be subjugated to the aim of creating a geometric/aesthetic scene.

Normal citizens and simple people would not necessarily be able to see the glorious scenic highlights of the palaces, parks, and gardens, as access was often restricted. They would be more likely to encounter such staged scenes in the churches, minsters and cathedrals. These were constructed in the heart of the cities, and were accessible to everyone, rich and poor alike. Even today, we are still fascinated by these grandiose and atmospheric interiors, which stage their stories as scenes that one can walk through. Paintings, saints' statues, altars, and crucifixes were used to tell the Christian sacred story. In Gothic cathedrals, glowing, colourful glass images could be seen in the naves, in the choir, and above the main altar. In the baroque churches, it is the altar itself that is presented to the delighted eyes of onlookers like a magic box, with cotton wool clouds, saints, and angels in flight.

What remains of it? Outside of the commercial zones of cities, the stage sets of shows, and our fairs, pleasure parks, sports venues, Olympic events, world exhibitions, theatres, and opera houses, the old magic of staging, with its connotations of transcendence, now primarily takes place in the world of cinema and television. Today, almost every living room is lit by a flickering screen, showing old Hollywood films, modern productions, series, and talk shows, along with the latest news. The Gothic choir windows and baroque theatrical altars showing tales from the Bible have been replaced by everyday stories and by filmic accounts of reality. The saints have undergone a transformation into celebrities, media stars, newsreaders and detective superintendents – people one will never meet in the flesh. The faces change every few years or so, in true democratic style. The news programmes tend more toward ominous reports of catastrophes, violent acts, and wars – rather like the Bible – but the uplifting stories are not forgotten. In the Bible, the happy ending is provided by the joyous resurrection on the last day; television, on the other hand, shows films on Friday evenings (rarely midweek) in which the cruelly separated lovers ultimately fall into one another's arms, like old Hollywood classics. A final kiss seals their shared entry into earthly happiness.

To look back even further, screens have replaced the primeval fireside circle. The lives of our Stone Age ancestors played out in caves. Winter nights, in particular, would have been cold and comfortless. The fire would give warmth and light, magically transforming the cold, damp cave into a comfortable space where flickering shadows played over the rough rocky walls. On the long winter evenings, gifted members of the clan would begin to paint on the walls. The anonymous cave would become a more personal living and sleeping space, sometimes even with an aura of animistic significance. So the story of »spatial stagings« had begun.

The same phenomenon can be seen in all early cultures. It did not stop with the painting of cave walls. Later, the entrances of huts and houses were hung with carvings and ornaments. Spirits and gods were invented, with stories told about them, and the vestiges of the dead and of ancestors, of nature spirits and of other unknown beings were documented on the walls and roofs of houses. Human beings wanted to give their incomprehensible, mysterious surroundings – as well as the wider cosmos and death itself – a colour of their own psyche and concepts. Ornaments, decorated rooms and buildings, and the painted and carved bones and skulls of prey animals and of the deceased: all of these create bridges between living individuals and the cosmos. It has always been true that only animals live in undecorated nests and caves.

Every culture in the world has produced its own rituals, its own staged spaces, its own atmospheric spaces, its own architectural decoration, and its own narratives. Some motifs are so strikingly familiar that one might al-

Hans Dieter Schaal

Zu meinen Arbeiten

Bei der Durchsicht meiner realisierten Arbeiten aus über 32 Jahren und der Photoauswahl für dieses Buch mußte ich – wie so oft – feststellen, daß Bühnenbilder und Ausstellungsgestaltungen mehr zu dem neigen, was ich »szenische Architektur« und »inszenierte Räume« nenne. Meine Vorliebe dafür konnte ich zwar in Entwürfen, Zeichnungen, Skizzen und Modellen ausdrücken, im tatsächlichen Architektur- und Landschaftsgestaltungsbereich jedoch nur selten verwirklichen. Im realen Alltag der Städte überwiegen, meist aus Kostengründen, die rein funktionalen Lösungen. Nur in den Einkaufsstraßen, Kaufhäusern und Malls werden »inszenierte« Räume und Bilder zugelassen, aber auch sie dienen einer klaren funktionalen Absicht: Ladenbesitzer und Mall-Betreiber wollen alle Passanten weder erschrecken noch künstlerisch beeindrucken, sondern in begeisterte, fröhliche Käufer verwandeln. »Inszenierungen« dienen als Lock- und Verführungsmittel.

Zu gewissen Jahreszeiten – etwa um Weihnachten herum – dürfen alte Sehnsüchte nach Romantik und märchenhaften Entrückungen aufblühen. Der Einkaufsbummel wird zu einem euphorischen Familienerlebnis gesteigert. Für wenige Wochen, manchmal auch für Monate, erhalten Straßenzüge, Fassaden, Schaufenster und Kaufhaus-Innenräume eine funkelnde Inszenierungsüberkrustung, deren Szenenbilder sich aus uralten christlichen Traditionen, Märchen und Filmen speisen. Schneeüberzuckerte Weihnachtsbäume, Weihnachtsmänner mit geschenkbepackten Schlitten, romantische Krippen, künstlicher Schnee und künstliche Eiszapfen, Lametta-Engel, lebendige Schafe und Esel versuchen eine Atmosphäre zu verbreiten, die mit dem normalen Alltag nichts mehr zu tun hat.

Auf Jahrmärkten, in Vergnügungsparks, in Varietés, unter Zirkuszeltkuppeln gehören diese Verzauberungen zum Alltag, allerdings ohne christliche Anspielungen. Übergänge zum Theater-, Opern- und Show-Bereich sind fließend. Durch phänomenale technische Entwicklungen lassen sich heute ganze Stadtbereiche in Klang- und Lichtdome verwandeln, deren Wirkung sich keiner der hunderttausend Besucher entziehen kann.

In den vergangenen Jahrhunderten neigten Adlige und reiche Bürger zur sichtbaren Repräsentation und damit zur Inszenierung ihres gesellschaftlichen Standes und ihres Vermögens. Sie bauten vornehm geschmückte Villen mit edel angelegten Gärten und Parks, sie verzierten ihre Hausfassaden mit Familienwappen, Ornamenten, Säulen, Skulpturen und Steinvasen. Und sie feierten üppige Feste mit Essensinszenierungen, Konzerten, Balletten, lebendigen Theaterbildern und nächtlichen Feuerwerken.

Natürlich konkurrierte ihr Verhalten mit den königlichen Spitzenleistungen auf dem gleichen Gebiet. Für viele Jahrzehnte galt Versailles als goldglänzendes Vorbild. Und Le Nôtres Gartenanlagen zeigten der zivilisierten Welt, was es heißt, die Natur mit geometrisch-ästhetischen Inszenierungszielen zu unterwerfen.

Normale Bürger und einfache Leute konnten in den oft unzugänglichen Schlössern mit ihren Parks und Gärten nicht unbedingt die glänzenden Inszenierungshöhepunkte sehen, sondern eher in den Kirchen, Münstern und Domen. Diese entstanden inmitten der Städte und waren jedem Bürger, ob arm oder reich, zugänglich. Auch heute noch wird man immer wieder gepackt von den grandios-stimmungsvollen Innenräumen, die als durchgehbare Märchenbilder inszeniert wurden. Erzählt wird die christliche Heilsgeschichte mit Gemälden, Heiligenskulpturen, Altären und Kruzifixen. In den gotischen Domen leuchten bunte Glasbilder im Kirchenschiff sowie im Chorbereich über dem Hauptaltar. In den Barockkirchen ist es der Altar selbst, der sich als Zauberkiste mit Stuckwolken, schwebenden Engeln und Heiligen den verzückten Augen darbietet.

Was ist davon geblieben? Neben den Zonen des städtischen Kommerzes, der Show-Bühnenbilder, der Jahrmärkte, Vergnügungsparks, der Sportstätten und Olympiaden, der Weltausstellungen, der Theater und Opernhäuser ist es vor allem die Welt der Kinos und des Fernsehens, in der die alte, zur Transzendenz neigende Inszenierungsmagie nachleuchtet. In fast jedem Wohnzimmer flimmert heute ein Bildschirm. Hier werden alte Hollywood-Filme gezeigt, aber auch moderne Filmproduktionen, Serien und Talkshows, dazu aktuelle Nachrichtensendungen. Aus den gotischen Chorfenstern und barocken Theateraltären mit den biblischen Märchen sind Alltagsgeschichten und filmische Realitätsberichte geworden. Die Heiligen haben sich in Prominente, Medienstars, Nachrichtensprecherinnen und Kriminalkommissare verwandelt, denen man leibhaftig nie begegnen wird. Sie wechseln, in demokratischer Manier, alle paar Jahre. Obwohl die Nachrichtensendungen, wie schon die Bibel, mehr zu bedrohlichen Berichten über Katastrophen, Attentate und Kriege neigen, werden die Heilsgeschichten nicht vergessen. In der Bibel bestand das Happy-End in der glücklichen Auferstehung am Jüngsten Tag, im Fernsehen fallen sich in den Freitagabendfilmen (selten am Mittwoch) – wie in den alten Hollywood-Klassikern – die getrennten Liebespaare in die Arme. Ein finaler Kuß besiegelt den Einstieg ins glückliche Erdenleben zu zweit.

Noch weiter zurückgeblickt, könnte man sagen: Bildschirme haben die uralt-archaischen Feuerstellen ersetzt. Das Leben unserer Steinzeit-Vorfahren spielte sich in Höhlen ab. Besonders die Winternächte waren kalt und trostlos. Das Feuer spendete Wärme und Licht und zauberte aus der kühl-feuchten Höhle einen gemütlichen Raum mit flackernden Schattenspielen auf den rauh-zerklüfteten Felswänden. An den langen Winterabenden begannen die künstlerisch begabten Mitglieder der Sippe, die Wände zu bemalen. So wurde aus der anonymen Höhle ein persönlich geprägtes Wohn- und Schlafzimmer, manchmal sogar mit animistischer Bedeutungsaura. Und die Geschichte der »Raum-Inszenierungen« begann.

Alle frühen Kulturen zeigen das gleiche Phänomen: Man bemalte nicht nur die Höhlenwände, sondern bedeckte später auch die Hütten- und Hauseingänge mit Schnitzereien oder Ornamenten, man erfand Geister und Götter, man erzählte sich Geschichten dazu und dokumentierte die Spuren der Verstorbenen und Ahnen, der Naturgeister und anderer unbekannter Wesen auf den Wänden und Decken der Hütten. Die Menschen wollten ihre unverständliche, rätselhafte Umgebung, den Kosmos und den Tod mit ihrem Geist und ihren Vorstellungen durchdringen. Die Ornamente, der Raum- und Bauschmuck, dazu auch die bemalten und beschnitzten Knochen und Schädel der erlegten Tiere und der Verstorbenen, stellten die Bindeglieder zwischen den lebenden Individuen und dem rätselhaften, schweigenden Kosmos her. Ungeschmückte Nester und Höhlen waren und sind nur bei Tieren anzutreffen.

most call them inborn images (like Jung's archetypes). Notwithstanding this, the first primal creations have given birth to differing cultures, each with its own unmistakable languages, signs, motifs, images, tales, and staged scenes. Developments also split along different lines. Some cultures were enamoured of images, and some were contemptuous of them – some were even actively hostile destroyers of images.

In the 20th century, the old images vanished under the onslaught of technological inventions and scientific insights, and the global awareness of individuals began a phase of explosive expansion. These developments and processes, however, have not really led to a convergence of cultures: instead, they have led them into life-threatening confrontations. Our city, home, and office environments have become more and more modern, and yet human brains are still dominated by archaic structures. All wars, both past and present, can be seen as the result of inborn aggressive reflexes dating back to the Stone Age.

However, it was not just the twin highly technologised catastrophes of two world wars that brought the threat of extinction to whole peoples and cultures. It was also the result of the militantly radical thinking of certain architecture theorists. One only has think, for instance, of the remarks of the Vienna architect Adolf Loos in his text »Ornament und Verbrechen« (»Ornament and Crime«) from 1908: »I have discovered the following insight, and offer it to the world: the evolution of culture is synonymous with the removal of ornamentation from functional objects.«

Certainly everyone knows that one must clear out a room every so often, removing old, superfluous rubbish. But anyone who throws away or burns all his personal things at such a time is essentially erasing himself, losing his memories along with the items that carry the memories. He is no longer an unmistakably distinctive individual who can look back on his own life.

Personal memories and a distinctive cultural history are a part of the individual's sense of self. The architecture of our homes, our workplaces and our cities are a natural part of this. Any theorist who shares Adolf Loos' belief that one can start from scratch is treading a false, inhuman path.

I am writing these lines in the year 2015. So, what is the position today? What meaning does the subject of »scenic architecture« and »staged-scene space« retain for us today? Each age redefines these terms. We are not operating in a zone governed by physics and mathematics, and no formula can prove that architecture or an architectural style is correct or incorrect. It is a question of taste. Opinions – and definitions – are constantly changing. Here, one sees the fundamental problem of all constructed architectures: their pronouncements, unlike those of the theatre, or the fashion world, have a tendency to be irrevocable. After only a brief time, they take on the appearance of historical documents, and become sometimes rather disruptive petrified remnants of a bygone age.

Life continues. New owners and tenants come along. Each new owner of a home is looking for a new atmosphere. When new occupants move in, the rooms are generally handed over empty, freshly renovated, and devoid of individuality. Rooms are given an unmistakable character by the addition of furniture, but also by images, photos, books, and the personal mementos of the people moving in.

Almost all modern architects build their structures and façades in a Bauhaus-inspired, coolly objective, unhistorically empty and technologically functional style that permits no highlights (except for advertising signs). This architecture appears to be modelled on hospitals, tax offices, and dental practices. The *Kunst am Bau* programme, run by public principals, represents the only (rather inadequate) effort to keep the old principles alive. Unfortunately, the results usually look like inevitably abstract patches. Nothing fits together, no story is told. Only the name plates by the doorbells and on the letter boxes tell us anything.

All previous eras – Romanesque, Gothic, Renaissance, Baroque, Rococo, Classicism, the Romantic era, Biedermeier, Historicism, the Makart style, Impressionism, Expressionism ... – appear to have been far richer in terms of architecture than the present day.

So, what about the situation today? This is what provides the starting point for this book. From the very beginning, I have always wanted my own architectural and spatial designs to tell stories with a dramaturgical tension, featuring motifs from literature, from film, and from the world of architecture. Not just on theatre stages and in exhibition rooms, but also on buildings, in parks, in gardens, and in landscapes, to interrupt all the expressionless, industrial and aseptic emptiness, and to restore to architecture all of the qualities that make it human and interesting: individuality, tension, and atmosphere.

The illustrations contained in this book bear witness to this endeavour. They are arranged chronologically, and they also show a specific progression: from large, exciting staged scenes at the beginning to ever-smaller assignments.

In recent years, I have been primarily concerned with memorials, which I have omitted here owing to their subject matter. Naturally, in the case of memorial sites, one can only create spatial situations that are appropriate to their specific requirements.

In 1983, when I was first able (and permitted) to use my stage set and exhibition designs to intervene into reality, there was little competition in these areas. I had been fortunate. Around the year 1980, Germany saw a conspicuous boom in staged, themed historic exhibitions. This trend is amply revealed just by looking at the events held at Berlin's Gropiusbau: there were major exhibitions dealing with the Prussians, Bismarck, the city of Berlin, the relationship between Moscow and Berlin, and the history of the Federal Republic (to mark the 50th anniversary). The numbers of design firms, architects, graphic artists, and media planners working in this field were increasing enormously. Computers and the internet were also becoming more important within all firms and exhibitions. Screens, projectors, and touchscreens were making their appearance everywhere. Completely unexpectedly – and not in accordance with anyone's wishes – the media revolution was breaking in upon society, and upon the world of exhibitions and of theatres.

In 1989/90, the historic change that came with the reunification of the two halves of Germany saw Berlin embark on its rise to become Germany's most popular tourist attraction. The same period saw the beginning of a decline in large-scale exhibitions. There was no longer any need to generate propaganda for the West and for »liberal capitalism«. Reality offered an abundance of material for narratives and images. The Expo 2000 Han-

In allen Kulturen der Welt entstanden eigene Riten, Bilder, Raum-Inszenierungen, Raum-Atmosphären, eigener Bauschmuck und eigene Erzählungen. Manche Motive gleichen sich so stark, daß man fast von angeborenen Bildern (den Jungschen Archetypen) sprechen kann. Trotzdem wuchsen aus den Ur-Kreationen verschiedenartige Kulturen mit eigenen, unverwechselbaren Sprachen, Zeichen, Motiven, Bildern, Märchen und Inszenierungen heran. Und die Entwicklungen spalteten sich in bilderliebende und bilderverachtende, ja bilderfeindliche und bilderzerstörende Kulturen auf.

Im 20. Jahrhundert überlagerten technische Erfindungen und naturwissenschaftliche Erkenntnisse die alten Bilder, und das globale Bewußtsein der einzelnen Menschen begann sich explosionsartig zu erweitern. Aber all diese Entwicklungen und Vorgänge führten zu keinen wirklichen Annäherungen der Kulturen, sondern zu lebensgefährlichen Konfrontationen. Die Welt der Städte, der Wohnungen und Büros wurde moderner und moderner, die menschlichen Gehirne jedoch sind noch immer von archaischen Strukturen beherrscht. Sämtliche Kriege, die vergangenen und die heutigen, können als angeborene Aggressionsreflexe aus der Steinzeit angesehen werden.

Aber nicht nur durch die hochtechnisierten Weltkriegskatastrophen waren jetzt ganze Völker und Kulturen von der Auslöschung bedroht, sondern auch durch die radikalen Kampfgedanken bestimmter Architekturtheoretiker. Man vergegenwärtige sich etwa die Ausführungen des Wiener Architekten Adolf Loos in seiner Schrift »Ornament und Verbrechen« von 1908: »Ich habe folgende erkenntnis gefunden und der welt geschenkt: evolution der kultur ist gleichbedeutend mit dem entfernen des ornamentes aus dem gebrauchsgegenstande.«

Sicher, jeder kennt das: Ab und zu muß man sein Zimmer aufräumen und alten, überflüssigen Müll entsorgen. Aber wer in diesem Moment alle seine persönlichen Dinge wegwirft oder verbrennt, löscht sich damit auch selbst aus. Er verliert mit seinen Erinnerungsbeweisstücken zugleich sein Gedächtnis. Er ist kein unverwechselbares Individuum mehr, das auf sein eigenes Leben zurückblickt.

Zum individuellen Ich-Sein gehören die persönlichen Erinnerungen und die eigene Kulturgeschichte. Natürlich auch die Wohnhaus-, Arbeits- und Stadt-Architekturen mit ihren Traditionen und verschiedenen Stil-Ausformungen. Jeder, der glaubt, man könne dies alles auslöschen, befindet sich auf einem unmenschlichen und falschen Weg.

Ich schreibe diese Zeilen im Jahr 2015. Wo stehen wir heute? Was sagt uns das Thema »szenische Architektur« und »inszenierter Raum« jetzt noch? Jede Zeit definiert die Begriffe neu. Wir bewegen uns in keiner physikalisch-mathematischen Zone. Die Richtigkeit oder Falschheit von Architektur und Architekturstilen läßt sich nicht mit Formeln beweisen. Geschmacksache. Meinungen und damit auch Definitionen ändern sich ständig. Darin erkennt man das Grundproblem aller realisierten Architekturen: Sie neigen (im Gegensatz zum Theater und zur Mode) zu unverrückbaren Behauptungen. Nach kurzer Zeit wirken sie wie historische Dokumente und werden zu manchmal störenden Versteinerungen aus vergangenen Tagen.

Das Leben geht weiter. Neue Besitzer und Mieter tauchen auf. Und jeder neue Wohnungsbenutzer sucht seine eigene Atmosphäre. Beim Einzug werden die Räume meistens leer, frisch renoviert und damit ohne Individualität übergeben. Mit den Möbeln, aber auch mit den Bildern, Photos, Büchern und persönlichen Erinnerungsstücken des Einziehenden erhalten sie erst ihre Unverwechselbarkeit.

Fast alle Architekten bauen heute – in der Tradition des Bauhauses – ihre Häuser und Fassaden in einem kühl-sachlichen, unhistorisch-leeren und funktional-technischen Stil, der keine Überhöhungen – außer Reklamezeichen – duldet. Krankenhäuser, Finanzämter und Zahnarztpraxen scheinen als Idealbilder zu dienen. Nur mit dem Kunst-am-Bau-Programm versuchen öffentliche Bauherren die alten Prinzipien notdürftig am Leben zu erhalten. Leider sehen die Ergebnisse zumeist wie hilflos-abstrakte Pflaster aus. Nichts paßt zusammen, nichts wird erzählt. Allein die Namensschilder bei den Klingeln und an den Briefkästen erzählen mehr.

Alle früheren Zeiten scheinen in ihren architektonischen Hervorbringungen weitaus reicher gewesen zu sein als die Gegenwart: Es gab die Romanik, die Gotik, die Renaissance, die Barockzeit, das Rokoko, den Klassizismus, die Romantik, das Biedermeier, den Historismus, den Makart-Stil, den Impressionismus, den Expressionismus. ...

Und jetzt? An diesem Punkt setzt das vorliegende Buch ein. Ich wollte von Anfang an mit meinen eigenen Architektur- und Raumentwürfen dramaturgisch spannende Geschichten mit Motiven aus der Literatur, dem Film oder der Werbewelt erzählen. Nicht nur auf Theaterbühnen und in Ausstellungsräumen, sondern auch an Gebäuden, in Parks, Gärten und Landschaften. Damit sollte die nichtssagende, industriell-aseptische Leere aufgebrochen und der Architektur wieder das zurückgegeben werden, was sie menschlich und interessant macht: Individualität, Spannung und Atmosphäre.

Die Abbildungen dieses Buches legen Zeugnis davon ab. Da sie chronologisch angeordnet sind, zeigen sie auch einen bestimmten Verlauf, nämlich den von großen, spannenden Anfangsinszenierungen zu immer kleiner werdenden Aufgaben.

In den letzten Jahren überwogen bei mir die Gedenkstätten, die ich aufgrund ihrer Thematik hier ausgespart habe. Selbstverständlich lassen sich in Gedenkstätten nur Raumsituationen herbeiführen, die dem besonderen Anlaß angemessen sind.

Als ich 1983 mit meinen Bühnenbild- und Ausstellungsentwürfen in die Realität eingreifen konnte (durfte), gab es wenig Konkurrenz auf diesen Gebieten. Ich hatte Glück. Um 1980 herrschte in Deutschland ein unübersehbarer Boom von inszenierten historischen Themenausstellungen. Allein der Blick auf die Veranstaltungen im Berliner Gropiusbau zeigt diesen Trend. Es gab große Ausstellungen über die Preußen, über Bismarck, über die Stadt Berlin, über die Beziehung zwischen Moskau und Berlin sowie über die Geschichte der Bundesrepublik (50-Jahre-Jubiläum). Gleichzeitig nahm die Zahl der Gestalterbüros, auch der Architekten, Graphiker und Medienplaner, die sich mit diesen Themen beschäftigten, enorm zu. Computer und Internet wurden zeitgleich in allen Büros und Ausstellungen wichtiger. Überall hielten Bildschirme, Beamer und Touchscreens Einzug. Die Medienrevolution brach, völlig unerwartet und von niemandem wirklich herbeigewünscht, über die Gesellschaft und damit auch über die Ausstellungs- und Theaterwelt herein.

1989/90 begann mit der Wende und der Wiedervereinigung der beiden Deutschlandhälften der Aufstieg der Stadt Berlin zur beliebtesten Touristenattraktion Deutsch-

nover can be seen as the last effort to buck this declining trend, but it was followed by a general loss of interest.

Within Germany, there were plenty of other factors contributing to this. Reunification cost far more money than politicians had expected or predicted. There were barely any instances of GDR firms being privatised or sold profitably. Most firms had to be abandoned and »wound up«. Some of them were sold for a single deutschmark – often to West German firms keen to eliminate competition from the East. The *Treuhand* – and therefore the West German state – accumulated many billions in debt. Some commentators believe the sum to be around 2 to 3 trillion. Additionally, countless former citizens of the GDR lost their jobs, became ill, took their own lives, or had to look for work in utterly unfamiliar surroundings. 3 million of them moved to the West.

The 11th of September 2001 shook America and the entire world. The dotcom bubble burst, and one banking crisis on top of another followed. No one could now stop the greed of the global stock exchange speculators, working through the medium of the internet. National governments were increasingly losing power and influence.

In Germany, the Greens were advocating for the abandonment of nuclear power and for the introduction of energy generation from renewables. Solar panels were conquering roof after roof – and in villages more so than in the major cities. Then there were the tensions and conflicts in the Middle East, in Afghanistan, and in Africa.

As the years went by, it increasingly appeared that the »Europe« principle might not, after all, be a model for success. The imposition of savings led to financial problems in many European countries, especially in Greece. Ever since 2008, banks have been paying practically no interest to savers. The euro has been quietly decreasing in value, without major resistance among the population. Meanwhile, the politicians try to persuade us that the situation is good.

So, what are the past and present-day consequences of all of this, with particular reference to our area of interest? Money has become more tight. Projects are getting smaller, and more lacking in visionary energy. Fewer and fewer people are interested in history, in museums, and in themed exhibitions in general. In particular, the younger generation, with their tablet computers and Facebook, tend to lead a historyless existence in an absolute today. The events of yesterday are old hat. Where it comes to mottos to live by and pleasure activities, it is egoism and affordably-priced event tourism that are in demand now. Anyone who wants to know more about something Googles it, or looks it up on Wikipedia. Practically anything can be researched through the new, media lexica search engines, in which entries are continually kept updated.

Suddenly, »stagings« in exhibition contexts came to an end. Today, the majority of museum directors are hostile to them, preferring to invest in valuable exhibits, or in online advertising. They are of the opinion that creating staged scenes brings no increase in visitor numbers, and is therefore not worth the effort. Although the number of design firms, and therefore the number of facets of expression, is rising, we are seeing – due to the stifling actions of financial backers and principals – an impoverishment in terms of styles, which can also be seen as a diagnostic expression of the real state of things.

Theatres and opera houses, like museums, now have less money. In eastern Germany, theatre companies have had to close, or merge. Today, there is barely any money to pay for stage sets. Some theatre directors dispense with a set entirely, choosing empty stages as the scene for their dramas and operas instead. Costumes and coloured lights have to suffice.

The same is true of public spaces: most investors only want to pay for what is absolutely necessary. Otherwise, the projected structure would be unprofitable; after all, it has to start making money as soon as possible.

At the same time, business is booming for architecture's few global stars. We should not be deceived by the impressive creations of Daniel Libeskind, Coop-Himmelb(l)au, Frank Gehry, Zaha Hadid, and Rem Koolhaas. All of them are buried within some metropolis or other, either near at hand or far away. Very few examples are to be found in Germany, and they play no role in the day-to-day life of normal cities. Their impact makes itself felt primarily through publications in architecture journals and internet portals.

Germany today still has 7,000 museums. Almost half of them are local or folklore museums, and only 10 % of them are dedicated to art. The rest are museums of a certain subject – museums of cars, stamps, beer mats, buttons, playing cards, winemaking, brooms, pipes, railways, aeroplanes, Zeppelins etc. Many of the smaller museums can barely get by on their entrance receipts and on their meagre public subsidies.

In view of all these factors, my battle for a revival of »scenic architecture« and »staged-scene spaces« may appear rather absurd. However, I regard these things as basic human needs, and for this reason I do not feel myself to be a Don Quixote.

Today, we are probably headed toward a world society, and therefore a mixing of cultures – and this is not purely a digital phenomenon, or one inspired by Hollywood. We can be sure that the next few decades will see – if for no other reason than to avoid fresh civil wars – the emergence of intriguing collages of widely differing worldviews and cultural images.

The results do not have to look like Las Vegas' Main Street – kitschy in places – or the midway of Munich's Oktoberfest. Nor do they have to be like castle-hotels hosting hearty medieval banquets, or the ethnically themed restaurants found all over the world. A great deal of other things are conceivable besides mosques, Buddhist temples, churches and monasteries, Chinese restaurants, and Bavarian beer parlours. Even taken by themselves, the numerous regional architectural styles of Europe, Russia, Africa, the Arab world, India, Japan, and the American continent represent a vast repertoire of inspirations. Each culture can learn from all the others, and welcome their influence as a form of enrichment.

lands, zeitgleich setzte der Niedergang großer Ausstellungen ein. Propaganda für den Westen und damit für den »freiheitlichen Kapitalismus« war nicht mehr notwendig. Die Realität bot reichlich Erzähl- und Bilderstoff. Eine letzte Aufbäumung gegen den Abwärtstrend könnte man in der Expo 2000 Hannover sehen, danach erlosch das Interesse.

Viele andere Gründe kamen in Deutschland hinzu. Die Wiedervereingung kostete weit mehr Geld, als die Politiker geahnt und vorausgesagt hatten. Kaum eine DDR-Firma wurde mit Gewinn privatisiert oder verkauft. Die meisten Firmen mußten aufgegeben und »abgewickelt« werden. Manche wurden für eine Mark verkauft. Oft an West-Firmen, die ihre Ost-Konkurrenz ausschalten wollten. Die Treuhand und damit der westdeutsche Staat machten viele Milliarden Schulden. Manche Beobachter sprechen von 2 bis 3 Billionen. Außerdem verloren unzählige Ex-DDR-Bürger ihre Arbeitsplätze, wurden krank, nahmen sich das Leben oder mußten sich nach neuen Jobs in völlig fremder Umgebung umschauen. 3 Millionen von ihnen wanderten in den Westen ab.

Der 11. September 2001 erschütterte Amerika und die ganze Welt. Die Dotcom-Blase platzte, und eine Bankenkrise jagte die nächste. Niemand konnte die Gier der global, mit dem Internet-Medium agierenden Börsenspekulanten mehr stoppen. Die nationalen Regierungen verloren zunehmend an Macht und Einfluß.

In Deutschland propagierten die Grünen den Atomausstieg und die Einführung erneuerbarer Energieerzeugung. Solaranlagen eroberten die Dächer, in Dörfern mehr als in den Großstädten. Dazu kamen die Spannungen und Kriege im Nahen Osten, in Afghanistan und Afrika.

Im Laufe der Jahre entpuppte sich das Prinzip »Europa« nicht unbedingt als Erfolgsmodell. Die Sparzwänge führten zu Finanzproblemen in vielen europäischen Ländern, vor allem in Griechenland. Seit 2008 bezahlen die Banken den Sparern so gut wie keine Zinsen mehr. Das Euro-Geld verliert still und leise, ohne großen Widerstand in der Bevölkerung, an Wert. Gleichzeitig reden die Politiker die Situation schön.

Was waren und sind die Folgen, auch für unseren Themenbereich? Das Geld ist knapper geworden. Die Projekte schrumpfen und verlieren an visionärer Kraft. Immer weniger Menschen interessieren sich für Geschichte, für Museen und Themenausstellungen allgemein. Vor allem die jüngere Generation neigt durch Tabletcomputer und Facebook zum geschichtslosen Dasein im absoluten Heute. Alle gestrigen Ereignisse sind kalter Kaffee. Egoismus und kostengünstiger Event-Tourismus sind die angesagten Lebensdevisen und Vergnügungen. Wer etwas mehr wissen will, googelt oder schaut bei Wikipedia nach. In den neuen, medialen Lexika-Suchmaschinen ist fast alles zu recherchieren. Und die Beiträge werden permanent aktualisiert.

Plötzlich war es mit den »Inszenierungen« im Ausstellungsbereich vorbei. Die Inszenierungsgegner unter den Museumsdirektoren überwiegen heute. Sie investieren ihre Gelder lieber in wertvolle Exponate oder Reklame im Internet. Der Aufwand lohne sich nicht mehr, denn die Besucherzahlen ließen sich dadurch – so ihre Meinung – nicht steigern. Obwohl die Zahl der Gestalterbüros und damit auch der Ausdrucksfacetten immer noch steigt, trat – ausgebremst durch die Geldgeber und Bauherren – eine stilistische Verarmung ein, in der zugleich ein Ausdruck der wahren Verhältnisse diagnostiziert werden kann.

Nicht nur den Museen wurde viel Geld entzogen, sondern auch den Theatern und Opernhäusern. Im Osten Deutschlands mußten Theaterbetriebe geschlossen oder zusammengelegt werden. Für Bühnenbilder gibt es heute kaum noch Geld. Manche Regisseure verzichten ganz auf eine Ausstattung und inszenieren ihre Theaterstücke und Opern auf leeren Bühnen. Kostüme und buntes Licht müssen genügen.

Genauso im öffentlichen Bereich: Die meisten Investoren wollen nur das Absolut-Notwendige. Ansonsten lohnt sich die geplante Anlage nicht. Sie muß ja so bald wie möglich Geld abwerfen.

Gleichzeitig boomt das Geschäft der wenigen Architektur-Weltstars. Man darf sich durch die eindrucksvollen Werke von Daniel Libeskind, Coop-Himmelb(l)au, Frank Gehry, Zaha Hadid oder Rem Koolhaas nicht täuschen lassen. Sie verstecken sich irgendwo in nahen oder fernen Metropolen. Nur sehr wenige Beispiele davon sind in Deutschland zu finden. Im Alltag der normalen Städte spielen sie keine Rolle. Ihre Wirkung entfalten sie vor allem durch Veröffentlichungen in Bauzeitschriften und Internet-Portalen.

In Deutschland gibt es heute immer noch 7000 Museen. Fast die Hälfte davon sind Heimat- und Volkskundemuseen, nur 10% sind Kunstmuseen. Der Rest: Themen-Museen – über Autos, Briefmarken, Bierdeckel, Knöpfe, Spielkarten, Weinherstellung, Besen, Pfeifen, Eisenbahnen, Flugzeuge, Zeppeline usw. Viele kleinere Museen leben mehr schlecht als recht von Eintrittsgeldern und geringen öffentlichen Zuschüssen.

Unter all diesen Aspekten scheint mein Kampf für eine Neubelebung der »szenischen Architektur« und der »inszenierten Räume« etwas widersinnig zu sein. Da ich darin ein Urbedürfnis aller Menschen sehe, fühle ich mich trotzdem nicht unbedingt wie ein Don Quichote.

Wahrscheinlich sind wir heute – nicht nur digital und vorbereitet durch Hollywood – auf dem Weg zu einer Weltgesellschaft und damit zu einer Vermischung aller Kulturen. Bestimmt werden in den nächsten Jahrzehnten – auch zur Vermeidung von neuen Bürgerkriegen – spannende Collagen der unterschiedlichsten Weltanschauungen und kulturellen Bilder entstehen.

Die Ergebnisse müssen nicht unbedingt aussehen wie in der punktuell kitschigen Main Street von Las Vegas oder in der Hauptachse des Münchner Oktoberfests. Auch nicht wie die Burghotels mit ihren deftigen Ritter-Festessen oder die folkloristischen Themen-Restaurants weltweit. Neben Moscheen, Buddha-Tempeln, Kirchen und Klöstern, China-Restaurants und bayerischen Bierstuben ist noch eine ganze Menge mehr denkbar. Allein die zahlreichen regionalen Baustile Europas, Rußlands, Afrikas, der arabischen Welt, Indiens, Japans und des amerikanischen Kontinents bieten ein großes Anregungsrepertoire. Jede Kultur kann von der anderen lernen und den Einfluß als Bereicherung begrüßen.